Overseas Research

Researchers in developing countries often find that the particular country in which they work presents a range of unforeseen challenges. Indeed, their ability to carry out effective scholarship is often highly dependent on these factors. The great differences between working in countries as varied as India, China, Bolivia, and Kenya can often come as a shock to the system. An ability to negotiate a bewildering array of cultural and logistical obstacles is therefore essential.

Overseas Research: A Practical Guide distils essential lessons learned by scores of students and scholars who have collected data and done fieldwork abroad. The authors fill the reader in on the many crucial pieces of advice: how to prepare for the field, how and where to find funding for one's fieldwork, issues of personal safety and security, and myriad logistical and relational issues that often define one's research experience abroad. As Barrett and Cason suggest, "Fieldwork is a sequence of decisions, some about the conduct of research, some about the conduct of life." The book focuses new field researchers' attention on that productive intersection, and includes many real-life accounts from experienced professionals whose own work abroad can inform those facing the field for the first time.

By encouraging researchers to think through the challenges of research before they begin it, *Overseas Research* will help prepare fieldworkers for the practical, logistical, and psychological considerations of very demanding work, help save valuable time, make the most of scarce financial resources, and enhance the quality of the field research. The book will also be of interest to undergraduates in subjects such as anthropology, economics, history, international studies, politics, and development studies.

Christopher B. Barrett is the Stephen B. and Janice G. Ashley Professor of Applied Economics and Management and International Professor of Agriculture, Cornell University, USA.

Jeffrey W. Cason is the Dean of International Programs and the Edward C. Knox Professor of International Studies and Political Science at Middlebury College, USA.

Overseas Research

A practical guide

Second edition

Christopher B. Barrett and Jeffrey W. Cason

Taylor & Francis Group

LONDON AND NEW YORK

First edition published by John Hopkins University Press 1997
Second edition published 2010
by Routledge
2 Park Square, Milton Park, Abingdon, Oxon, OX14 4RN

Simultaneously published in the USA and Canada
by Routledge
270 Madison Avenue, New York, NY 10016

Routledge is an imprint of the Taylor & Francis Group, an informa business

Typeset in Sabon
by Keystroke, Tettenhall, Wolverhampton
Printed and bound in Great Britain
by TJ International, Padstow, Cornwall

British Library Cataloguing in Publication Data
A catalogue record for this book is available from the British Library

Library of Congress Cataloging in Publication Data
Barrett, Christopher B. (Christopher Brendan)
  Overseas research: a practical guide / Christopher B. Barrett and
  Jeffrey W. Cason. – 2nd edn.
    p. cm.
  Includes bibliographical references and index.
  1. Social sciences – Fieldwork. I. Cason, Jeffrey W. II. Title.
  H62.B338 2010
  300.72'3 – dc22   2009036830

ISBN10: 0–415–77833–6 (hbk)
ISBN10: 0–415–77834–4 (pbk)
ISBN10: 0–203–82627–9 (ebk)

ISBN13: 978–0–415–77833–6 (hbk)
ISBN13: 978–0–415–77834–3 (pbk)
ISBN13: 978–0–203–82627–7 (ebk)

We dedicate the second edition of this book
to Clara and Gail.

Contents

Selected bibliography **140**

Field narrative boxes

Contributors of field narratives

Carolyn Barnwell was a Thomas J. Watson Fellow in 2007–8 and is now the Communications and Outreach Coordinator at Brighter Planet working on climate change solutions.

Gretchen Bauer is a professor and also the department chair of political science and international relations at the University of Delaware.

Carolyn Behrman is an associate professor of anthropology at the University of Akron and director of the cross-disciplinary *Active Research Methods* teaching laboratory.

Karen Booth is an associate professor of Women's Studies at the University of North Carolina at Chapel Hill.

Steve Boucher is an associate professor of agricultural and resource economics at the University of California at Davis.

Mary Clark is an associate professor of political science at Tulane University.

Jason Cons is a PhD candidate in development sociology at Cornell University.

Andrew Dillon is a postdoctoral fellow at the International Food Policy Research Institute.

Heidi Gjertsen is an economist consulting for Conservation International and NOAA Fisheries Service.

Laura Hammond is a senior lecturer in development studies and a member of the SOAS Food Studies Centre, the Centre for Migration and Diaspora Studies and the African Studies Centre at the School of Oriental and African Studies at the University of London.

Darren Hawkins is a professor and also the department chair of political science at Brigham Young University.

Francisca James-Hernández is a Mellon Postdoctoral Fellow in the Humanities at the Dept of Ethnic Studies at the University of California at Berkeley.

Christian Lentz is a visiting scholar in sociology at Duke University.

Annemie Maertens is a PhD candidate in applied economics and management at Cornell University.

Dan Maxwell is an associate professor and the research director for the food security and livelihoods program at the Feinstein International Center at Tufts University.

Hope Michelson is a PhD candidate in applied economics and management at Cornell University.

Karuna Morarji is a PhD candidate in development sociology at Cornell University.

Sudha Narayanan is a PhD candidate in applied economics and management at Cornell University.

Kasia Paprocki is research and program manager at the Goldin Institute.

Tyler Priest is a clinical professor and the director of Global Studies at the Bauer College of Business at the University of Houston.

Will Reno is an associate professor of political science at Northwestern University.

Jerry Shively is a professor and associate department head of agricultural economics at Purdue University.

Michael Sullivan is an independent scholar and works at a "Fortune 500 company."

Aili Tripp is a professor of political science and gender and women's studies as well as director of the Women's Studies Research Center at the University of Wisconsin-Madison.

Greg White is a professor of government at Smith College.

Foreword to the second edition

Brian Whalen

"The Guide is definitive. Reality is frequently inaccurate" wrote the late British comic writer Douglas Adams in his novel, *The Restaurant at the End of the Universe* describing his earlier work, *The Hitchhiker's Guide to the Galaxy*.[1] This book by Christopher B. Barrett and Jeffrey W. Cason is the definitive guide to overseas research, and will provide those who use it with the information and tools they need to deal with the complexities and shifting realities that are part and parcel of the overseas research situation. While they do not journey as far as the end of the universe, they do prepare researchers for every possible cultural setting and challenge across the globe.

Research conducted in international settings poses unique challenges for students and scholars. Knowing how to prepare for and adequately carry out the logistics of research projects can be a daunting task. The myriad issues that one must consider range from how to select a site to securing the proper equipment to being sensitive to the needs of the host culture and society. This book covers every aspect of international research and in doing so helps to raise the quality of overseas research.

A primary audience for this book should be undergraduate and graduate students and the faculty with whom they collaborate, or who supervise their research. Undergraduate study abroad research activity has expanded in recent years as a wide variety of field research programs have developed as independent education abroad programs, or as an added element to the traditional study abroad program model.

Indications of this expansion can be seen in the growth in popularity of the Undergraduate Research Awards sponsored by the Forum on Education Abroad. In 2005 the Forum initiated these Awards to honor students who conduct the nation's best research as part of their study abroad programs. Winners present their research at the Forum's Annual Conference, which has always been a highlight of the gathering. In the four years of the competition over 200 applications have been submitted, signaling the growing popularity of research abroad as an important and legitimate aspect of education abroad. Finalists have been invited to submit their research papers to *Frontiers: The Interdisciplinary Journal of Study Abroad*. Together with the Forum, *Frontiers* has published these research papers in a series of three volumes documenting excellence in student overseas research.[2] Faculty advisors and on-site resident directors and supervisors have written corresponding short essays reflecting on the significance of each student's work.

While student research continues to grow and develop, accepted guidelines for conducting such research are not always commonly shared. The Forum Standards of Good Practice for Education Abroad are the most authoritative set of standards for the field of education abroad and include a section addressing "Internships and Field Research". The Standards stress the importance of embedding field research within a rigorous academic program with adequate supervision, requirements, monitoring, assessment, and adherence to ethical guidelines, particularly when research involves human subjects.[3] These Standards help institutions and provider organizations improve the quality of education abroad programs that offer field research opportunities; the authors of this book provide step-by-step guidance on how best to meet these standards.

The information that forms the backbone of this *Guide* is gleaned from researchers in the field. Surveying those who have conducted overseas research and what lessons they have learned is an ideal approach for identifying best practices; what works, and what doesn't. This method personalizes the material presented, and gives the reader the sense that he or she is "stepping into the shoes" of the overseas researcher. By presenting and analyzing case studies and presenting vignettes written by experienced researchers, Barrett and Cason describe best practices for all areas of conducting overseas research in a very appealing, user-friendly format.

A strength of the *Guide* is the way that the authors have re-created key "decision points" that are faced by researchers in the overseas research process. They do this by relating not only success stories, but also lessons learned from failures and common obstacles that have been encountered by others. Readers will value especially Barrett and Cason's view that overseas research unfolds in unexpected ways. It does not always follow a set course, no matter how effective the planning might be. The authors have many examples of how to deal with changes in mid-stream and how to prepare for the unexpected.

Another noteworthy aspect of this *Guide* is the authors' reflections on the important connection between the researcher's personal life and the objective research that he or she carries out. There is, perhaps, something distinctive about international research in the way that it often becomes deeply personal for the researcher. The same can be observed with students who study abroad and with faculty involved in leading education abroad programs. The authors show how this personal passion for international education should be embraced, and how it can advance the research in productive ways rather than hinder the outcomes. The dividing line between the personal and professional is often blurry for the international field researcher who is challenged to navigate through a different culture and society while maintaining an objective distance on their topic of study. The authors note that the "personal and professional concerns are difficult to disentangle. Personal misery or stress too often ruins the research experience, while a joyful experience often contributes to outstanding fieldwork, if only invisibly. We strongly advise indulging one's personal passions in selecting a research site." Barrett and Cason reveal through their examples and analyses how to make the best of the challenges of being personally challenged while professionally engaged in an international setting.

Also to be appreciated is the way in which the authors advise that researchers should be sensitive to the needs of the host cultures and societies in which field research is conducted. Students, faculty, and researchers abroad must realize that their presence and activities do not exist in a vacuum, and that their hosts deserve a debriefing regarding outcomes of certain types of research projects. As Barrett and Cason note, "For those doing survey work, it is a nice, but too rare, courtesy to present some basic findings in a simple closing talk to the subject community. This can provide useful feedback to the researcher as well as to the subjects."

This *Guide* provides advice that is both theoretical and practical. It covers the context for conducting research abroad and the supporting logistics, as well as tips for employing excellent research methodologies to meet the challenges of various international settings. Ultimately, one of its most important contributions will be to help to improve overseas education and research by advocating that these activities be closely connected to the curriculum and by encouraging faculty and student collaboration.

In the years ahead, curricula at our colleges and universities will continue to become increasingly internationalized, education and research abroad will continue to expand for both undergraduate and graduate students, and faculty research conducted overseas will become more commonplace. Our global society will demand this and much more from our institutions as we seek to understand our rapidly shrinking globe in all of its marvelous complexity. Barrett and Cason have provided us and our students with a map to guide our way.

Brian Whalen, President and CEO,
The Forum on Education Abroad

Notes

1 *The Restaurant at the End of the Universe*, Del Rey Books, 2005, p. 37.
2 These Special Issues, as well as all past volumes of *Frontiers*, are available online at www.frontiersjournal.com
3 *The Standards of Good Practice for Education Abroad*, Forum on Education Abroad, Carlisle, PA: 2007.

Preface and acknowledgments for the second edition

When *Overseas Research* was first published in 1997, it was meant to target an audience of graduate students and junior faculty who would be conducting field research in the social sciences and humanities for the first time. That first edition was highly successful, selling its entire print run and earning strong reviews. The volume has been featured on course syllabi in a wide range of programs at quite a variety of colleges and universities in multiple countries, including (among others) Boston University, Columbia University, Georgetown University, Indiana University, MIT, Princeton University, San Francisco State University, UC-Berkeley, University of Akron, University of London, University of Oxford, University of Pennsylvania, University of Southern California, University of Toronto and the University of Wisconsin-Milwaukee. We have been gratified to see and hear how many people have found the volume useful.

When the first edition went out of print, several colleagues and students immediately encouraged us to update the book and release a second edition. On reflection, we realized that enough had changed about the practice of fieldwork in the intervening dozen years – especially due to the rapid growth in numbers of undergraduate students conducting overseas field research, enormous changes in information and communications technologies, and heightened concerns about personal safety – that a second edition might add value to our initial effort.

This second edition updates the original edition and includes much new material. We added a distinct chapter on safety and security issues. We went back to all the contributors to the first edition as well as about four dozen additional scholars with recent fieldwork experience – including a good number who went overseas as undergraduates – and elicited their comments on the first edition and posed additional questions to them. This yielded several new field narratives in this edition, as well as many helpful updates and added nuance throughout each of the chapters. Looking back at what we wrote a dozen years ago, when we were both at the early stages of our academic careers, was at times entertaining, though we were heartened to see that much of the advice we gave then still held true.

Given our method of writing this book, drawing heavily on the collective experience of many researchers from across disciplines, institutions and parts of the globe, the project would have been truly impossible without the generous cooperation of many individuals. In addition to those listed among the contributors of field narratives, Carolyn Brown, Doug Brown, Sommarat Chantarat, Nicole Conti, Chad Futrell, Brian Hoyer, Amichai Kilchevsky, John Maluccio, Beth Medvecky, Sharon Osterloh, Rachel Rosenfeld, Liz Ross, Ria Shroff, and Andrei Takhteyev all offered valuable comments for this second edition. We are grateful that Dr Brian Whalen, President and Chief Executive Officer of the Forum on Education Abroad (http://www. forumea.org/) generously agreed to author the foreword to this second edition, given the Forum's commitment to encouraging more undergraduate research abroad.

This second edition benefitted enormously from invaluable assistance from Erin Lentz and Veronica Palladino, who carefully and constructively reviewed the first edition with a youthful eye towards useful updates that the aging co-authors might miss and meticulously compiled comments and contributions for this second edition. The staff at our publisher, Taylor & Francis (under their Routledge imprint), have been extremely helpful. Rob Langham and Emily Senior skillfully shepherded us through this second edition's publication.

As with the first edition, we reserve our final and most heartfelt thanks for our families. Their support and patience inspire us and they have often helped infuse our own fieldwork with unforgettable moments . . . mostly joyful ones! Brendan, Mary Catherine, Joanna, Julia and Elizabeth tolerated their father's extended absences and the rigors of writing. The trips on which they have accompanied him have always been the most wonderfully memorable ones. Through it all and over exceptionally long distances over more than two decades of marriage, Clara has repeatedly made Chris's international work possible and worthwhile. Although vicarious, her field experiences have been no less arduous and invigorating than Chris's.

Elias, Sophia, Gabriel, and Gail were able to experience the field firsthand with Jeff for a year in Brazil, and taught him the challenges and rewards of bringing an entire family to the field. They also made the fieldwork experience more relaxing, realistic, and enjoyable. There is nothing like having a family abroad to make you slow down and think through what you are really doing. It was also a joy to see all of them learn so much while abroad – linguistically, culturally, personally – which will surely be a high-light of their lives.

Foreword to the first edition

Kennette Benedict

This book came out of a project to test whether knowledge and perspectives from countries outside the United States can contribute to a deeper understanding of regional security dilemmas and strategies for international cooperation. With financial support from the John D. and Catherine T. MacArthur Foundation, junior and senior scholars from the University of Wisconsin-Madison created an interdisciplinary learning community. Faculty and students took up the challenge on interdisciplinary training and research in peace and international cooperation with unusual energy and commitment.

At least two assumptions guided the effort. First, to investigate the dynamics of conflict and cooperation in civil or regional conflicts, we need a range of disciplinary tools. Economic, social, cultural, and technological factors, among others, contribute to conflict, so people trained in corresponding disciplines can offer useful methods of investigating these complex social processes. Second, students and young professionals bring fresh approaches and important, if sometimes uncomfortable, questions to the study of regional conflicts and global trends; they can challenge conventional wisdom and stimulate new understanding.

While we all expected that graduate students' research and fieldwork would be enriched by the project, none of us could have anticipated the book that Christopher Barrett and Jeffrey Cason have authored. Drawing on field research experiences of students at the University of Wisconsin and of those supported by the Ford Foundation through the Social Science Research Council's International Predissertation Fellowship Program, this book provides valuable guidance for those heading to the field for the first time.

The authors address that gray area of research experience between participation and observation. Anyone who has been immersed in a new culture to learn about the complex patterns of interaction is familiar with the tension between the roles of observer and participant. Important insights can be gained through direct observation as a participant in a foreign setting. And for many researchers, participant observation in the field forms the basis of a lifelong commitment to research in a particular country or region beyond their own. Successfully straddling the line between participant and observer may be the single most important skill students can obtain in the course of dissertation field research. As Barrett and Cason suggest, "Fieldwork is a sequence of decisions, some about the conduct of research, some about the conduct of life." It is at the intersection of conducting research and living life that some of the most penetrating insights may come. This book will help focus researchers' attention on that productive intersection.

This collection of experiences will also prepare first-time field researchers in the practical ways for what is always an unnerving, messy, and difficult time. Such preparation is particularly important in an era of reduced funding for field research in the social sciences. The steady erosion of financial resources for overseas travel, scholarly exchanges, and social science research is taking its toll on the opportunities for direct field experience in societies outside the United States. Because of limited funding, it is incumbent on those who are able to obtain money to travel, study, and live abroad to use it carefully and wisely. Scholars no longer have the luxury of spending precious time "reinventing the wheel" to do effective field research. That is another reason that *Overseas Research* should prove to be an important contribution; it can prepare young fieldworkers in the practical, logistical, and psychological considerations of very demanding work, help save valuable time, and make the most of scarce financial resources.

This publication grew out of the experiences of many individuals, financially supported by a range of private philanthropic and public governmental sources. Without the initiative of the students and the intellectual guidance of faculty and administrators at the University of Wisconsin, however, the knitting together of these experiences in a community of learning would not have happened. The practice of students mentoring other students is not new, but the extent to which the Wisconsin program encouraged a self-conscious and open sharing of information and experience is unusual. Hopefully, this initiative will inspire others to contribute, even at a time of declining resources, to cooperative and effective training in international social sciences.

Kennette Benedict, Director
Program on Peace and International Cooperation
John D. and Catherine T. MacArthur Foundation

Preface and acknowledgments for the first edition (updated)

It is customary to begin a preface by acknowledging how the final product would have been impossible without the help of many others. As the reader will soon discover, this book is exceptional in the degree to which direct and concrete assistance was provided by many individuals. Indeed, the project would have been unfeasible without others' quite active participation. Those listed as contributors provided thoughtful passages as detailed responses to an open-ended questionnaire distributed by the co-authors, and we thought them so compelling that we included them verbatim in text boxes listed in the table of contents. They and many others took time to review and correct a draft manuscript. We thank them for their time and thoughtfulness. In addition, many fellows in the Social Science Research Council's International Predissertation Fellowship Program released copies of reports on their fieldwork to use. For their cooperation in a wide variety of ways, we thank the following individuals: Regina Abrami, Robert Andolina, Helen Ruth Aspaas, Sarah Babb, Patrick Barrett, Clifford Bob, Charla Britt, Susan Burgerman, Cameron Campbell, Karen Sue Crehore, Lisa Fischler, Thamora Fishel, Leslie Gray, Armando Guevara-Gil, Janice Harper, Soren Hauge, Stephen Herschler, William Kandel, Beth Katz, Stephen Kay, Morgan Yih-Yang Liu, Steve Marquardt, Walter Molano, Ann Marie Murphy, Albert Park, Janet Roitman, Chuck Schmitz, Denise Stanley, Marc Stern, Keiko Tanaka, Twila Tardif, Merle Wallace, Margaret Weigers, Jurgen Wiesmann, and Chris Woodruff. We thank Ellen Perecman and Amy Chazkel of the SSRC for facilitating this cooperation and for their enthusiastic support. Richard Lobban and Leonardo Villalón kindly shared materials from a panel on research issues in West Africa they convened at the November 1994 annual meeting of the African Studies Association in Toronto. In addition to those who contributed with their fieldwork experience, Patricia Gray and Jon Moris provided substantial suggestions, especially for the bibliography.

The idea for the book grew out of the MacArthur/SSRC scholars program at the University of Wisconsin-Madison, housed within the Global Studies Research Program (GSRP). We thank Michael Carter, Jim Riker, and Barbara Stallings for their facilitation and support of this program. We especially thank David Trubek for providing the resources and moral support to turn our proposal into a project, and Carol Torgeson for out-standing administrative support. Laurie Brown, Sandy Lee, and especially Ruby Vasquez of the Economics Department at Utah State were unceas-ingly helpful and patient in preparing the manuscript, and Mary Duffy provided help at a moment's notice on the Vermont end of the project. In addition, the MacArthur Foundation's support for the consortium between the University of Wisconsin, the University of Minnesota, and Stanford University provided additional contributors, and the consortium's June 1995 Summer Institute in Madison provided a wonderful opportunity to present the first draft of the manuscript for comments and suggestions. We thank Kennette Benedict of the MacArthur Foundation for her support of the consortium's activities. The skilled staff at the Johns Hopkins University Press have made the publication process uncommonly pleasant. We especially thank Henry Tom, Miriam Tillman, and Hillary Reeves for the care they have given our work.

Finally, our families deserve credit, thanks, and gratitude for supporting our own fieldwork and putting up with the time demands of this book. It is an understatement to say they have been an inspiration and support. Brendan and Mary Catherine tolerated their father's extended absences and, along with Joanna, the rigors of writing. Through it all and over excep-tionally long distances, Clara has made Chris's international work possible and worthwhile. Although vicarious, her field experiences have been no less arduous and invigorating than Chris's. Carolina Menéndez has come to the field with Jeff on several occasions and provided concrete help in the research process. More important – and this became particularly obvious when the field was faced alone – she provided the companionship that made living in the field a joy. Carolina also provided quite a tangible contribution to the book, as she compiled the index for the first edition.

1 Introduction

Every year a great number of enthusiastic, well-trained young scholars set out on their first overseas research project and, with an awesome display of energy and creativity, reinvent the flat tire. To some extent their difficulties are inevitable. Moreover, the war stories we all bring back from the field often add zest to the rigors of scholarly research. Yet it is too often equally true that projects drag on needlessly, data sets become corrupted, time runs out, scarce funds are squandered, and young researchers become demoralized by missteps and obstacles that might have been avoided.

We believe that a fair proportion of such missteps and obstacles are due not to poor formal training, but to a lack of field-tested advice on practical matters. Anyone who has set out to collect data in "the field" knows the gnawing feeling that previous methodological study is of limited value in the successful conduct of field research. When such research is in a foreign culture, the doubts and worries inevitably multiply. What a researcher often yearns for is something between a technical manual on data collection and a chatty travel guide. This book aims to begin to fill that void.

We have gathered information and experiences gleaned from more than 200 scholar-years of overseas fieldwork, reported directly to us or to funding agencies (when scholars authorized release of the relevant reports). As one fellow wrote to the Social Science Research Council (SSRC), "There is a large amount of information available on practical and academic issues that grad students frequently face when heading to the field. The problem is that this information is scattered and difficult to obtain." It is our hope that this volume makes it easier to gain access to a large portion of such information.

We qualify our ambitions, however, by recognizing that familiarity with the research site is an important and highly idiosyncratic part of mastering the field methods relevant to any particular project. And tastes vary, so one person's preferred approach may not suit another person's. Still, there are cautions, techniques, and tips that have demonstrated wide applicability across disciplines and continents. We pull many such threads together here in the hope of alleviating some of the stress felt by overseas researchers, especially those embarking on their first major project, and of thereby helping improve the quality of field research. Our dream is that copies of this book will have dog-eared pages stained with airline coffee and covers worn from frequent rubbing against the rucksack frames of researchers who become avid and productive observers of the diverse societies that span the globe.

Much of what this book covers falls under the heading of common sense: learning where you are and about the people with whom you live and work, thinking through the ramifications of your words and deeds, and anticipating and preparing for contingencies. With the exception of exploring means of dealing with particular problems that might be faced in executing a research plan (Chapter 7), we avoid technical issues of research methodology (e.g. sampling, questionnaire design, conducting oral history interviews, participant observation) for three reasons. First, disciplinary courses thoroughly cover both theoretical issues that motivate fieldwork and methodological issues on how to gather and exploit the data collected; and the chasm between hypothesis and test is bridged formally by a substantial body of research-methods literature. Second, given the multiplicity of methods in the social sciences and humanities, integrating these disparate approaches far exceeds our abilities and ambition. Third, it is not altogether clear that most of a field researcher's time is really spent on research. In a perhaps exaggerated claim, Nigel Barley says that scarcely 1 percent of his time in Cameroon was spent conducting research, with 99 percent dedicated to "logistics, being ill, being sociable, arranging things, getting from place to place, and above all, waiting" (Barley 1983: 98). Even for those graced with an abundance of pure research time in the field, mundane activities merit attention in their own right. Yet no disciplinary courses, academic advisers or published literature meets the palpable need of inexperienced researchers for current, field-tested advice on practical issues of planning, preparing, and conducting fieldwork.

We hypothesize that young students and scholars mentored in mundane matters have more enjoyable and productive research experiences. This belief was born of our own experiences in the MacArthur Scholars Program at the University of Wisconsin-Madison, where we first came up with the idea for the first edition of this book in 1994. Wisconsin's MacArthur scholars enjoyed unusually fertile cross-disciplinary sharing of perspectives on theory, methods and, especially, the day-to-day details of research abroad through formal workshops, less formal roundtables, and informal social gatherings. By sharing practical insights gleaned from their own research experiences, scholars already returned from the field routinely aid newer scholars in the design, preparation, and execution of successful projects. Although it is impossible to establish how much value this environment has added to the research of a select group of capable and energetic young scholars, the cumulative results suggest that the whole has exceeded the sum of its parts.

In putting together the first edition of this book we surveyed approximately 150 scholars funded in the early and mid-1990s by the MacArthur Scholars program at Stanford and Wisconsin or the Social Science Research

Council's International Predissertation Fellowship Program. In preparing this current, second edition, we surveyed an additional 56 scholars and students who had done fieldwork abroad in recent years, including faculty at various ranks and many students who had done research abroad as undergraduates. Including a few others who volunteered their experiences, this second edition now includes the collective wisdom of 85 scholars and students representing a wide variety of disciplines across the social sciences and humanities. The contributors did their research abroad as tenured or tenure-track faculty, as graduate students doing PhD or MA thesis research, or as undergraduates doing independent or collaborative research. Collectively the respondents undertook extensive field research in more than four dozen countries in Africa, Asia, the Caribbean, Europe, Latin America, the Middle East and Oceania. This group's experience in funding overseas research was outstanding. Virtually all received significant funding for their research, including major research programs such as Fulbright or Fulbright-Hays, the Inter-American Foundation, the Institute for the Study of World Politics, the Midwestern Universities Consortium for International Activities, the National Science Foundation, the Rockefeller Foundation, the Social Science Research Council, the Tinker Foundation, Wenner-Gren, or the West Africa Research Association. Many also received research funding from their home institutions, which recognized the important work they were doing. Moreover, these research projects have borne scholarly fruit. The faculty who have contributed to this book have published scores of articles and many books based on their fieldwork. The undergraduate contributors have also published articles based on their fieldwork abroad, or have gone on to graduate school or to positions in the policy or NGO worlds where they have put into practice the insights they gained while doing fieldwork abroad. Many of the contributors maintain quite active international research agendas. It is likely that the impressive collective record of the contributors owes something to the opportunities presented for informal and formal sharing of insights on how to design, execute and survive overseas research projects. This book is an attempt to share those fruits with a broader audience in similar circumstances.

It is essential, for at least two reasons, that the reader keeps in mind that this volume is a compilation of many individuals' lessons learned from overseas field research. First, this is no cookbook; not all points are relevant or appropriate to all research settings. We aim to jog the memory, good judgment and conscience of overburdened field researchers, not to substitute for those resources. Second, we do not want the mass of detail that follows to intimidate or discourage anyone, especially not newcomers to the field. Just as no one scholar alone could have offered these insights, so too is it unlikely that any one person can (or should) follow completely the guidelines offered in this volume. Read and digest it in bits, as needed, with the full appreciation that all the contributors themselves have to some degree stumbled through fieldwork, but ultimately emerged the better for the experience.

The two of us, although experienced, are not experts at fieldwork; we serve mainly as rapporteurs for those who have learned by doing. It may be useful for the reader to understand how this book came together, both in its first edition and in this new, second edition. For the first edition, we solicited comments using a detailed outline of open-ended questions corresponding to the book's structure, and encouraged respondents to add their own questions. The cooperating scholars thereby defined the book's content, if not entirely its structure. Many also released to us copies of related reports they had filed with grantsmaking organizations. We then drafted the volume, relying extensively on scholars' solicited and unsolicited responses, and recirculated the full text to those researchers, as well as to external reviewers, for correction, enhancement, and refinement. This second round of comments guided final revisions. We quote directly and liberally from contributed remarks, both to represent experiences accurately and to provide a sense of the group's wide-ranging (and sometimes conflicting) lessons learned.

For the second edition, we decided to expand the scope of the book to include undergraduates in addition to our originally intended audience of graduate students heading out to do fieldwork for the first time. The simple reason is that undergraduates are now commonly embarking on field research for the first time in much the same way that graduate students were in earlier years. From 1997, when the first edition was published, until the 2006–7 academic year (the most recent data available), study abroad for US-based students has increased 143 percent, to nearly a quarter of a million students annually (Institute of International Education 1998; 2008). Many of these more mobile students are conducting research abroad, in a wide variety of contexts. There has also been a trend toward more rapid growth in non-traditional (i.e. non-European) study abroad; over this same period, study abroad in Africa, for example, increased from just over 2,500 students to more than 10,000, and in China from just over 1,600 to more than 11,000.

To expand the scope of the book, update its advice, and add new sections (on security, for example, see Chapter 6), we followed a strategy similar to that of the first edition; we surveyed a new group of researchers for their input. This time we included undergraduates, graduate students, and faculty, and asked some targeted questions as well as eliciting general feedback on the first edition. As a consequence of this additional feedback, we were able to add important new content – especially on the role of modern information and communications technology, on personal and physical security, and an enlarged bibliography – and expand on the kind of advice contained in the first edition.

We decided against an edited volume so as to maximize the integration of related insights and minimize redundancy. Perhaps, more important, synthesis facilitated structuring the presentation so as to correspond to the chronology of an overseas research project: beginning with site selection and funding, continuing through pre-departure preparations, field activities, and repatriation, and ending with considerations that endure long after the return from the field. Fieldwork is a sequence of decisions; some about the conduct of research, some about the conduct of life. This volume presents many decision points commonly faced by researchers overseas, roughly in the order in which they usually arise. We provide some guidance on how others have resolved such decisions, both satisfactorily and unsatisfactorily. The basic approach is thus to identify prospective decisions, map out alternatives, and, where the evidence and logic are strong, proffer prescriptions.

It should be self-evident that one cannot divorce the practice of data collection from the physical and social environment within which data are collected. For that reason, interpenetrating professional and personal matters are addressed together throughout the volume. This process involves not only the management of time, talents, and resources but also some of the difficult ethical choices researchers must routinely make. Overseas research (especially in low-income societies), which regularly places northern elite fieldworkers among sometimes desperately poor people in alien cultures, frequently elicits profound experiences in which issues of personal conduct can be of singular importance.

We do not pretend to have run perfect research projects. Indeed, some of this volume's most valuable offerings derive from costly and embarrassing failures, many of them our own. Nor do we claim to have all the questions, much less the answers, concerning practical matters of overseas research. After all, there are always new developments, and there is no substitute for exercising good judgment. Yet we believe good judgment can be honed by anticipating and reviewing prospective challenges and decisions, some of which are identifiable from the past experiences of other researchers. This book should help in that endeavor. Field research is not deterministically controlled by an investigator – that would not only prove dull, but would probably suffocate illuminating discoveries born of chance – but neither is it a fatalistic endeavor. One exerts considerable influence over one's research environment by the resolution of particular issues that frequently arise. In the nine chapters that follow we present a compendium of one group's guidance on many such issues that comprise the potentially marvelous experience of overseas fieldwork.

2 Identifying a site and funding source

Fieldwork begins at home, and the portion at home is often no less taxing than that abroad. Indeed, many scholars find the first step in a research project the hardest. The initial challenges, sometimes daunting, that we explore in this chapter include selecting a site and funding a project. We identify the issues to consider in the earliest stages of defining and funding an overseas research project. In identifying these issues, we describe some common obstacles you can expect and suggest how to navigate successfully around them.

With the important exceptions of research projects that are subsumed within a larger research program and evaluations of specific events or projects, the process of site selection generally precedes courting funding agencies.

Site selection

It is perhaps obvious that you need to have a research site before conducting overseas field research. After hypotheses are preliminarily defined, you must decide where, when, and how to investigate the question(s) at hand. Sometimes – for undergraduates on study abroad programs, for example – the site selection was made when you decided to study on a particular program in a particular place. For many others, however, choosing a site can be a difficult enterprise as you try to balance personal and professional objectives, often in a state of extreme ignorance. The "homemade" decisions that result substantially influence the course of subsequent fieldwork and, thus, are not to be taken lightly. At the same time, it is inevitable that you will make many choices with limited information and will inevitably regret some of them. Focus on the big things and try not to sweat the small stuff.

A site must be chosen because the *place* interests you. However, you must also consider the feasibility and future marketability of the research project as well as personal and family needs or preferences. In addition, timing can play a critical role. Obviously, the appropriate weighing up of alternative professional and personal criteria depends on a wide variety of individual circumstances.

The appropriate balance among these criteria does, nonetheless, vary some-what predictably across disciplines and methods. For instance, researchers fielding a formal survey and aspiring to conduct quantitative data analysis leading to general policy implications typically need to give more attention to how the location or timing of research might affect sample frame construction or respondent participation rates. On the other hand, researchers who are undertaking a qualitative ethnography – where they are likely to be in the field for an extended period – may be less concerned with the precise timing of the research. In some cases, once you decide upon a topic and country for research, the site becomes obvious. A scholar studying decision-making within the central state bureaucracy must almost inevitably be located in the national capital. A researcher studying a particular sort of economic or cultural activity must obviously go to where such activities are prominent. Historians must generally go to wherever the appropriate documents are archived.

But site selection is often far from obvious. One of the co-author's field-work on the effects of economic liberalization on rural food marketing and production could have been conducted in any one of thousands of towns and villages in a host of countries. Especially when the physical location of an appropriate site is relatively unimportant, considerations of timing, feasi-bility, marketability, and personal preferences weigh heavily in the final choice of a research site.

There are many temporal issues to consider in site selection. Those doing rural research must pay attention to agricultural calendars, which dictate seasonal labor, migration, and expenditure patterns. Rainy seasons can seriously disrupt travel or necessitate extra expenditure for an appropriate vehicle. If one is sensitive to the heat or cold or especially vulnerable to seasonal allergies, timing may matter for personal comfort and health. Political or cultural events, such as electoral campaigns or uncommon festivals, can heavily influence the environment in which you collect data. The month around or following Christmas is "down time" in many Christian cultures. In Islamic cultures, the month of Ramadan can accelerate respondent fatigue in daytime interviewing, forcing much research into hours of darkness. It is important to identify local holidays and vacation periods in establishing your fieldwork schedule.

Young scholars often overlook the crucial timing issue of sequenc-ing fieldwork and preparatory literature review at the home institution. Anxious to get to the field, many do not leave sufficient time to prepare at home before departing overseas. Although it may appear obvious, many researchers learn the hard way the value of a complete and careful reading of the relevant empirical and theoretical literature available at the home institution before departure. Do not take for granted high-speed, low-cost internet access of the sort students routinely enjoy in North America and Europe. While you might be fortunate and have adequate connectivity to access your home institution library and other electronic resources from abroad, in many places this remains more difficult, expensive, or both. It remains essential to nail down research questions and to have reviewed basic background materials before reaching the field. This saves valuable field time otherwise spent collecting superfluous secondary materials or trying to pin down the research question. One researcher left for the field only one day after completing his PhD preliminary examinations, having done only a skimpy literature review, and ended up with disastrous results. He reports that as a consequence, "I had only a superficial understanding of the place, and I wasted enormous amounts of time and effort collecting materials that were indeed available at home. This also had a very negative impact on my ability to narrow my research topic. As a result, I consider this to have been my greatest mistake, and if there is anything I will make sure to do in the future, it will be to avoid a repetition of this experience." Greg White echoes this point in the narrative below.

Box 2.1 The value of preparing at home

You can't overestimate the value of being thoroughly familiar with the resources at your home institution. Furthermore, with the advent of the internet, one is increasingly able to map what's available in the field. I was in the field for the first time in 1990, essentially the pre-internet era, and I was convinced that my home university's library would not have volumes from the early 1970s of the superb *Annuaire de l'Afrique du Nord*. As a result, I spent hours poring over the volumes in the archives in Tunisia and France. Of course, I "wept" when I returned to Madison and found that the library did, indeed, have a full complement of volumes.

Greg White

Another scholar, who did take time to prepare well in advance of his departure, emphasizes the "key importance of adequate prior training in field techniques," which can be central to establishing the feasibility of the initial research design and adapting it accordingly. Others noted that an examination of past theses and dissertations based on research in the targeted country can provide valuable leads to data sources as well as obscure but useful archival materials.

In general, the more empirical the nature of a research project, the more focused site selection tends to be at the outset, thus making the research task simpler. Yet researchers with such an early, clear vision of where they will do fieldwork may start off with an insufficiently focused theoretical framework, which can lead to aimless empiricism and frustration. As a corollary, the more theoretical the issues to be investigated, the less precise the researcher's initial thoughts about an appropriate site, thus making site selection more challenging. For scholars of this stripe, a preliminary visit to the field is especially valuable. (We address exploratory research trips in the next section.)

This brings us naturally to considerations regarding the broader aims of the study, that is, to the desired degree of specificity of the research project, which is often correlated with its empirical or theoretical roots. Prior research about the selected area can be of enormous value, providing baseline data or, in the best of cases, a foundation for constructing a rare longitudinal study. One anthropologist was pleased to find that "the ethnohistoric and ethnographic record for [his] area [was] sound, allowing the insertion of [his] research interests into a broader analytical map." Preexisting primary data sets likewise influenced site selection for a number of other, especially quantitatively oriented, researchers who seek to build on pre-existing data to study patterns over time.

The feasibility of the project must be established clearly and early along at least two dimensions. First, is the prospective research site relevant to the hypotheses you wish to test? Can you get sufficient variation along a number of different axes to control confounding variables and isolate the relationships of interest? Do you have the necessary language skills to fulfill the research objectives in the research site? (We will address language and language training later in this chapter.) Second, can the research design be implemented logistically and administratively in the proposed site? If inter-regional (much less international) communication or transport is important, can the infrastructure support your project requirements? Simple issues, like the existence of appropriate scale maps or electricity, can matter enormously to the feasibility of a particular research design. Don't assume everything you will need exists; look into it carefully. Administratively and intellectually, it is often advantageous to have a host country collaborator, so you may want to consider identifying local researchers conducting similar work. Not only can they provide uncommon insights into your research question, but the cross-cultural collaborations can be wonderfully enriching experiences, both personally and professionally.

As a researcher, your nationality influences the feasibility of a given project. "Insider" researchers (i.e. host country natives) often have more extensive contacts and multiple means of satisfying logistical needs. In particular, nationals of the host country generally meet less resistance in securing research clearance on potentially inflammatory subjects than do foreigners, whom the government might consider insensitive to the social and political environment. Razavi (1993) made this case strongly in describing her research in Iran. A researcher's gender can be a factor as well. Several women reported sensing they had an easier time negotiating bureaucratic obstacles, albeit for the unfortunate reason that many governments do not take female researchers seriously enough to consider them a potential threat.

Having raised the issue of insider research, we should note it often carries less status professionally. Many grantsmakers will not fund research in the country of origin or in peripheral communities within the United States or its territories. Furthermore, some potential employers, especially academic departments, look down upon those who return to their native lands for research as if they somehow lacked the courage to step away from the familiar. In doing so, they ignore the fact that familiarity can be a valuable asset in research. But, as Sudha Narayanan relates, it can also pose unanticipated challenges.

Box 2.2 When "overseas" is home

There is a sense in which going "home" to do fieldwork makes things easy. There are few adjustment issues and one only has to re-acquaint oneself with [the] minutiae of daily living. Help is always forthcoming from old friends and relatives, who, in my case, were scattered generously across my field area. However, this posed other difficulties that I was utterly unprepared for. After more than a decade away, my presence in India was seen as a break that was long overdue, and my first months were soaked up attending weddings, funerals, births, birthdays, babysitting, etc. I recouped quickly enough to get my work back on track, but it did take considerable effort keeping my personal and professional diaries separate, and to disabuse all of the notion that I was on a long holiday.

It was not just family and friends whose expectations I had to negotiate. In the field survey I conducted of farmers in Tamil Nadu, my shared linguistic and cultural background encouraged my respondents to accord to me the status of an insider, not typically reserved for a student researcher from abroad. This "kinship" meant that I was drawn into their lives in a way I couldn't have anticipated – farmers often sought my advice on their children's career choices, information on cultivation practices in the US, on how their daughters could be more confident, on employment options in the city and in some cases, they shared personal tragedies and sorrows. Interviews that ought to have taken forty-five minutes invariably lasted hours. I was richer for the experience, but the responsibility of engaging with them as an insider often left me overwhelmed, not to mention the sheer demands it made on my time. Under these circumstances, it was always difficult to keep things simple or spare.

To anyone going to do fieldwork in a familiar location, I would recommend a strategy to manage others' expectations; and, if not that, calibrating your own expectations from your fieldwork to accommodate the juggling of insider-outsider hats.

Sudha Narayanan

The future marketability of one's research almost invariably figures prominently in site selection, if only subconsciously. Francisca James-Hernandez makes this claim eloquently in her contribution. Advisers and colleagues invariably recommend sites for their "policy relevance," prestige, likely connections for finding a future job, or potential to publish the results obtained there. Young researchers almost invariably, and probably wisely, tend to heed such advice.

Box 2.3 Choosing the research site

Consciously or not, I submit most researchers consider status in choosing their research topic, field site, theoretical orientation, and the population studied. I suspect most deny it, however, believing academe is fundamentally meritocratic, functioning on the free trade of ideas. Even so, it's only realistic and pragmatic to be aware of how ideas are rated better or worse in the intellectual marketplace. The choice of field site and others made throughout the research process have an impact on the possibilities of getting an attentive or knowledgeable academic adviser (if you're a student), getting published (including access to publishers), getting academic appointments, getting grants, getting tenure, and so on. All of these and other considerations are the cultural capital of the field. This said, I don't advocate a choice of field site based exclusively on maximum career returns. High cultural capital can be deceptive and is not necessarily nurturing of one's intellectual creativity nor of that intangible rarely acknowledged in academe, one's happiness.

In my view, the choice of field site is, ideally, one of passion. Where do you feel most passionate as a researcher? What place gets you excited, warms your cheeks at the thought, and, above all, inspires you to write? What place and population will get you through months of 100-degrees-plus-weather, intestinal parasites, sexual assaults, tarantulas for the arachnophobic, or whatever else it is that will make fieldwork precarious, dangerous, boring, frightening, enraging, stupefying, or any of the other potential myriad obstacles that will, inevitably, arise from time to time, if not constantly?

Francisca James-Hernandez

As Hernandez notes, "passion" is a powerful attractor (or repellent) in site selection. This accounts in part for the common phenomenon of the children and grandchildren of immigrants returning to their ancestral lands for study abroad and initial field research, and of overseas volunteers (e.g. Peace Corps) returning later as scientists on a research project. Personal and family concerns are undoubtedly the most understated determinants of research location and timing. Scholars are often reluctant to acknowledge anything other than scientific or academic bases for site selection. Nonetheless, such concerns exert enormous influence over the ultimate choice, and properly so. Heading to the field with a pregnant wife or a husband not quite finished with his degree is hard on everyone. Finding a place where both partners are excited to work is difficult. Taking small children to malaria- and plague-infested areas borders on recklessness, and living in a polluted and perhaps hostile city has its own problems. Evacuation tends to be simpler and quicker for a single adult than for a family in a research area subject to civil strife. Personal and professional concerns are difficult to disentangle. Personal misery or stress too often ruins the research experience, while a joyful experience often contributes to outstanding fieldwork, if only invisibly. We strongly advise indulging one's personal passions in selecting a research site.

Many established scholars report that their initial choice of sites was guided by personal interests, and only the refinement of site selection was determined by "professional" criteria. The choice of country in which to undertake fieldwork is commonly influenced by dependents' language skills, professional situation, past experiences and lifestyle. Indeed, one researcher remarked, only partly in jest, that "the only valid criteria for choosing [sites] are an abiding fondness for the food, music, and people!" Conversely, several people reported not choosing prospective sites because of serious concerns about health conditions, security, or the availability of activities to engage accompanying dependents.

Researchers with accompanying families understandably place a great premium on finding a place where their dependents can be happy. In the case of couples each undertaking research, besides the obvious need to identify a site in which both parties share a keen interest, a key criterion is realistic means to balance childcare and research demands. Some couples alternate duties, others find live-in domestic and childcare help, which is commonly very reasonably priced and high quality in low-income countries. For some researchers, happiness is equated with North American conveniences, thereby sharply narrowing the range of prospective field sites. One contributor who took a wife and child to the field freely admitted that, in site selection, "my real reasons were personal, but academic theoretical reasoning matched my practical needs perfectly – a rare stroke of luck." We suspect his site selection process to be far more common than most researchers publicly acknowledge.

That said, some disciplined souls swallow hard and, despite knowing the difficulties of a site, consciously choose it anyway because of its outstanding research attributes. Some reported that it took a year or more to acclimate to the discomforts of living in, as one researcher described it, "a sort of equatorial hell, a malaria-infested lowland farming center that had been destroyed in the war and then left forgotten for a decade and a half." In our observation, unaccompanied fieldworkers are by far most likely to exhibit the grit necessary to make such a choice and to see it through successfully.

Exploratory research trips

The problem of site selection has multiple levels. Once you have decided on a country in which to do your research, the choice of the particular city, region, and subpopulation remains. An exploratory trip can help enormously in pinning down a site by permitting the selection process to be subdivided into stages. In the first stage, you can consider the broad questions of topic, general timing, and host country (or a small set of contiguous alternatives) at your home institution. But if given the chance to make a preparatory visit to the host country, you can put off the particulars of location and timing (which are influenced by issues of feasibility and personal needs, resources, and preferences) until learning more about the alternatives firsthand.

Thus, the best recommendation we can offer is, when at all possible, do exploratory research before making a longer-term commitment. Indeed, those researchers we consulted considered this such a crucial part of a good research plan that several recommended funding this initial trip as an out-of-pocket expense, if necessary. Consider it an investment bearing handsome dividends. Several weeks in the field at this stage – or, in the case of an undergraduate looking for a place to spend several weeks, a long weekend or half-week wisely spent – can save several months later on. Moreover, grantsmaking organizations generally look favorably upon in-country experience, established collaborative affiliations, and the clearer sense of understanding of the important questions and feasible research designs that comes from an exploratory research visit.

Thankfully, there are means by which a young scholar can finance exploratory research trips without resorting to credit card stress. A wide variety of foundations and research organizations run small grants programs easily found in an internet search or by checking with faculty with relevant research interests. Most major research universities and many Title VI area studies programs in the United States have regular competitions for small travel grants, which are designed to provide seed money toward more substantial extramural funding. Those involved in overseas consulting may have the opportunity to reroute flights through a potential research locale and to take a few weeks to scout out the site, and thus, gather necessary materials, determine the feasibility and appropriateness of the research, and establish the necessary contacts. Two of our respondents did this quite successfully, "dropping by" Ethiopia and Togo on the way back to the US from Zimbabwe and Morocco, respectively.

An exploratory research trip of a month or two (although even just a few weeks, even several very-full days, may suffice) permits you to establish contacts and locate potential collaborators; to find institutions with which you might wish to affiliate; to dig through the archives, literature, and data already available in-country; and to investigate living conditions. Under-graduates on study abroad programs can use their time abroad to familiarize themselves with their research sites, as well. All researchers can return home to revisit the relevant empirical and theoretical literature and to investigate subjects previously overlooked but revealed by the light of the recent trip to the field. In the case of undergraduates, they may end up simply staying on after their study abroad experience to do research, so learning as much as possible about the site – and communicating with faculty advisers back home about what one finds, and the next appropriate steps – will make their (usually shorter) research experience more productive.

An exploratory visit inevitably builds contacts that prove useful later on. For example, one of the co-authors was able to line up enumerator teams for interviews and training before returning to the field because a preparatory visit generated names and field survey experiences with a number of prospective assistants. In some cases, preparatory time in a country even allows you to establish contacts in the very communities to which you will return for the full-blown research project.

More commonly, although collaborative relationships are most often established via email or post, preparatory visits can provide an especially valuable opportunity to establish professional affiliations and secure research clearances, which are important, if not requisite, in the competition for scarce funding. When at all possible, get letters while still in-country since an "out of sight, out of mind" mentality prevails as much among foreign bureaucrats and scholars as it does at home. Like it or not, personal connections and contact matter enormously to the conduct of official business the world over.

Often the choice of institutional affiliation is limited because of the paucity of host country research organizations, the narrowness of the research topic, or both. But where there is some latitude, different strategies can help you choose among alternative collaborators. One is to select the institution with the best reputation, either for funders or to informants, to whom one might present a letter of introduction on institutional letterhead. An alternative is to affiliate with the organization that seems most likely to provide the greatest support to the proposed research project. In the best of all possible worlds, these two strategies coincide; but often they do not. The real key is to establish a solid personal connection with at least one person in the organization, someone you can approach for advice and assistance when unsure of how to proceed in navigating local obstacles.

Many researchers interviewed for this book were able to get logistical support (e.g. an office; a computer; a vehicle; access to phone, fax, photo-copier, internet, library, or lab), valuable assistance in negotiating bureau-cratic obstacles, or academic guidance from host country sponsors. Most importantly, such an active affiliation can mean that research does not take place in a vacuum; it has palpable links to host country academic and policymaking circles. A host country affiliation can thus be a boon to the overseas fieldworker. One researcher rightly reminded us to "consider exactly what you as a researcher can give to your collaborators on a daily basis, since you are likely to take quite a bit in the course of your visit."

Another contributor noted that while settling into Bangladesh, she offered her "time (and ability to write in English) to [her hosts] as a way to repay them for their help. . . . This work was a nice way to get to know folks in the office and how they were thinking about related issues."

Still, many prospective host country sponsors are understandably wary of foreigners looking for an institutional or organizational affiliation. Too often, skills, data, and information flow in one direction, and host country scholars often tire of such parasitic experiences. So, too, do their years of exposure to pontificating foreign "experts" sometimes lead to understandable impatience with visiting researchers. Some sponsors are suspicious of the motives of visiting researchers and project onto them commercial ambition, partisan political agendas, or an intelligence-gathering function, regardless of whether such motives exist. Moreover, more than one host country scholar has had brilliant research ideas pirated, without acknowledgment, by foreign visitors privileged with superior access to research funds, publications and eminent co-authors or mentors. In some places such experiences (and opportunism) have prompted local institutions to demand substantial fees or a share of one's research grant money in exchange for the privilege of affiliation. Under such circumstances the costs of affiliation might exceed the benefits, so you should clearly establish the requirements for affiliation before committing to a professional relationship.

The shorter the period spent in-country on a preliminary site visit, the more important it is to inform people in advance of the impending longer visit and, where possible, to prearrange meetings. In general, talk to as many people as possible in the time available. One researcher reported having built up the list of useful people to meet by getting the names of two or three more people from each person he met. He, like several other respondents, gave a one-page summary of his research project to those who were interested. Inexpensive electronic storage makes it easy to carry documents on a USB stick or a hard drive, or to leave them on an accessible website for downloading when needed in order to share with those who show an interest. Although they are often overlooked in North American and European universities, business cards remain essential for making introductions in many developing countries where such formalities are still a common currency and a crucial signal of seriousness of purpose.

Often it is possible to bring home secondary data and work through it carefully between field periods. Armed with secondary data and interview notes from an exploratory research trip, you can refine theoretical models and empirical methods with the aid of advisers and colleagues who may be harder to reach from the field. If you are able to collect field questionnaires used by other researchers as well as other survey instruments, you can often prepare a first draft of your primary data collection materials (ready for pretesting) before returning to the field.

Several scholars observed that it is a good idea to undertake an exploratory research trip even if you have been to the site before. If your previous exposure has not been in a research context, prior acquaintance may engender a false sense of familiarity. Even a brief exploratory research trip allows you the opportunity to read the newspapers, listen to radio programs, and talk to people to see if the original research design properly identifies the issues and actors. Northern scholars commonly approach questions in an unfamiliar society with tools and understanding gleaned from places with which they are more familiar, but which may be inappropriate or irrelevant. This can be dangerous because placing problems in a specific context is crucial to producing analysis that is both accurate and relevant.

The preparatory visit also allows you to get a feel for living conditions at the research site. By noting what goods and services are available in satisfactory quality, quantity, and price, you can quickly identify which items to bring for the longer haul and which to leave at home. You can also learn the idiosyncrasies of local telecommunications – internet access, cell phone reception, etc. – and can work out appropriate contingency plans. Especially for those who leave family at home, this can save considerable expense and anxiety in the long run. While global cell phone service and Skype or other Voice Over Internet Protocol services make it easy to maintain contact across vast distances today, it still pays to check out the communications infrastructure carefully when making an exploratory visit. In most cases, the best approach is to buy a local GSM-capable phone and SIM card, and then buy pay-as-you-go units. A local phone number is indispensible for setting up appointments and being reachable, and is valuable for personal security (see Chapter 6).

Likewise, learning about the health situation and services, housing options, and host country banking services can preempt many of the crises that inevitably consume inordinate amounts of research time. Just making a few contacts and becoming familiar with the physical layout of the place, the food, and the ambiance can go a long way toward relieving the inevitable anxiety you experience in advance of departure for the "real thing." As Devereux and Hoddinott (1993: 10) noted, "One major anxiety all fieldworkers feel is the urge to get the research under way as soon after arrival as possible (to 'hit the ground running'), and the temptation to rush things is that much greater if the ground has not been cleared in advance." In one way or another, virtually all scholars we spoke with stressed that some prior acquaintance with "the field" is highly desirable, if not essential, to a successful research experience overseas.

In short, a preliminary trip allows you time to test the feasibility of the original research design and to rethink carefully the entire project before committing fully to its execution. Often the feasibility, relevance, and desirability of an extended period committed to research in a foreign location can be properly evaluated only from first-hand, practical experience. Several scholars who did not undertake a short preliminary visit desperately wished they had. At a minimum, the site(s), timing, questions, or methods of research get fine-tuned according to current conditions prevailing in the host country. Moreover, it is not uncommon for researchers to revise their projects dramatically after an exploratory visit, even to settle on sites in countries other than those initially visited or on completely different topics. This can forestall the sort of panic experienced by Will Reno and facilitate a productive transition, such as he made (see below).

Box 2.4 Changing the research topic in midstream

One month into my research sojourn in Sierra Leone to study the politics of agricultural reform, a crisis over my research agenda was brewing. Any six-year-old small child on the street knew that "reform" in Sierra Leone was a joke. Fourah Bay College students laughed at my research plans. "What *is* the real story here?" I asked. "Corruption," was the reply. I fell into a depression. My research proposal contained only the lies I read in official documents I collected in the US before my departure. Here I was, thousands of miles from home, months to go in my stay, and I [would have to] return home with no dissertation topic, quit school and beg for quarters in front of the university library.

It hit me as I was walking along a path in the nearby forest preserve: study how the country really works. A simple proposition, to be sure, but difficult to operationalize, since most politics takes place through manipulation of black markets. So, I set out to study how political leaders use black markets to manage rivals and reward supporters, a topic that eventually netted me a book contract. The end result, however, bore virtually no resemblance to the original research proposal.

Will Reno

Many (especially young) researchers carry with them to the field romantic notions about foreign societies. An exploratory research trip often serves a valuable purpose in disabusing you of distracting preconceived notions, thus permitting more careful study and understanding of the complex realities of the site. One respondent reported back to the SSRC:

Another area in which my "thinking" is still evolving as a result of my year in Central America has to do with the positional politics of being a "First World" leftist intellectual studying peripheral societies. While I have always been aware of the obvious paradox involved in studying subaltern groups and societies from the privileged vantage point of the well-supported US academy, I found myself facing a more personal aspect of this problem last year. I came to realize that, on an emotional level, I did not like Costa Rican culture or Costa Rican society. . . . In short, I found myself . . . projecting onto [Costa Ricans] the qualities I disliked most about North American culture. As I came to understand this – and the contradictions of such a position – I think I gained not only a keener insight into the illusions of leftist romanticism, but also a more nuanced understanding of real popular aspirations, at least in Central America.

You cannot presume to do more than scratch the surface of a foreign culture in a visit of a few weeks or months, but becoming aware of some subtleties can help to prepare you for the field and can help in research design.

Language training

Although it was once taken as gospel that aptitude in the local language was a prerequisite to fieldwork, scholars now dispute whether competence in the native language of a research site is necessary or even desirable, given the considerable time and money spent on language study. Devereux (1993: 44) makes the case for this position:

> Language impinges on both major components of fieldwork – the research exercise and the social or personal aspect. From both points of view, there can be little doubt that fluency is preferable to total incomprehension. . . . If acquiring fluency were an entirely costless procedure, therefore, there might be a case for insisting that this should be a prerequisite for every fieldworker.

> But learning the language is a "data collection exercise" in its own right, and the investment of valuable time and intellectual energy in acquiring this knowledge should be assessed alongside the imperative to collect other types of data. Even if the benefits of fluency are sizeable, this time and energy might be better employed doing other things.

An exploratory research trip provides probably the single best gauge of the level of language ability needed to execute the planned research. Moreover, language study can often be combined with other objectives (such as those described above) in an exploratory research trip.

For those who need or want to undertake intensive language study before field research, there remains the important choice of whether to study language in-country or at home, perhaps at an intensive language program such as those run in the summer at any number of colleges and universities. Most experts assert that an immersive environment is the key to learning the language well. Programs that insist on twenty-four-hour-a-day dedication to the target language – no English allowed! – win high marks from virtually all commentators.

Ironically, overseas training might not always be the best choice. Although it carries the benefit of allowing a person to live in an environment where the target language is also a living language, other problems can arise. Texts and instructors can be of low or uneven quality. Instructional methods frequently emphasize rote learning, especially in difficult languages. One really needs a practical approach to learning the language if the objective is to put it to use colloquially in support of one's research project. Unfamiliarity with the environment often induces foreigners to spend time together, so that study overseas may actually undermine the attainment of true language immersion. Moreover, unless your skills in the target language are already far better than most locals' skills in English, many conversations naturally turn to English, either because the native speakers are trying to be helpful or because they want to practice their English.

While language skills are clearly crucial for much overseas research, you may not need to be fluent. Establish up front the level of fluency needed to implement your research design successfully and the most effective means to reach that level. Moreover, establish clearly which language is necessary; the official language of a country is often inappropriate to a particular regional site. At a minimum, learn basic greetings in the local language(s) of the people with whom you will interact. The gesture is almost always appreciated and often generates a good laugh! Many research subjects, and even reasonably well educated local research assistants, may not be truly fluent in a second or third language if they typically operate in their mother tongue. Keep in mind that insufficient language skills are one of the primary reasons projects fail, and funding agencies will be much more likely to turn down grant proposals if these skills are inadequate. Knowing the language skills you need commonly takes some local interaction and good advice from others with previous local research experience. In the end, your research project will determine the linguistic skills and competency that you need to have. When really understanding your research site at a deeper level is essential, you are likely to need greater linguistic skills so that locals will be able to communicate with you in their native language. Such greater linguistic abilities will allow you to pick up on nuances that are inaccessible in translation. In other cases, such detailed understanding of the research site may not be as crucial, and you may prefer to spend your energy and training on other things.

In practice, many researchers develop minimal necessary competency in the appropriate language(s) and hire a native speaker translator for essential interviews. One typically wants research subjects to speak in whatever language they find most comfortable, both out of respect and because accuracy tends to increase when the primary speaker is most comfortable in the language of the conversation. It is important, however, to give very careful instructions to interpreters; many people will naturally summarize rather than translate verbatim. Know what you need from your respondents and your translator and then communicate that to the field assistant clearly.

Finding funding

Selecting a site and finding funding are often interrelated, with funding frequently depending upon the choice of a particular research site and, in some cases, a site being chosen in part to attract funds. The process of financing even a relatively meager budget is rarely easy.

"Apply early, apply often." "My advice to students is to 'create' your way to success, by any means imaginable, unconventional, exploratory, or otherwise." "Even if the chances seem slim, *apply*!" These are typical replies we received to questions about how researchers found funding for their projects. The point is clear: Make time for fundraising. You make your own breaks in the scramble for overseas research funding.

Leave no stone unturned. Remember that the apparent raison d'être of a multitude of organizations is to write checks to eager and capable young researchers. The tedious task of plowing through the huge grants registers is inevitable. Online search engines can expedite the process, but a certain amount of tedium is inevitable. Send simple, enthusiastic emails or letters to any prospective sponsor that seems even remotely interested in the research topic. Do *not* send form letters, but instead study the criteria of each agency in order to understand and respond to their stated interests and objectives. This does indeed take a great deal of time, but it is a necessary investment if you wish to finance a thorough research project. Such inquiries generally elicit prompt replies indicating whether funds are available, and, if they are, applicable deadlines and instructions. In rare but delightful cases, donors impressed with one's proposed research send a small, unconditional grant simply in reply to thoughtful queries. These small sums might not fund an entire project but can be marketed to donors offering bigger grants as a sign of others' confidence in the value of the research project. Moreover, smaller grants can provide valuable discretionary funding (to hire assistants, rent a vehicle, or buy useful equipment such as a cell phone or a laptop computer) in the event that a more substantial award comes through.

We note that the process seems somewhat more difficult and the range of grants for which you are eligible somewhat narrower in the case of nonresident aliens (some grants are exclusively for citizens of the granting country) or those undertaking research in one's home country. Contrary to myth, few substantial research grants (as opposed to student fellowships) are available only to minorities, much less only to those from disadvantaged areas of the world.

Overall, the process of identifying prospective sources of research funding and applying for grants generally takes many months and in many cases must be initiated a year or more before you intend to leave for the field. Funding agencies then typically take several months to review applications and announce funding decisions, sometimes not leaving researchers with much time before departing for the field, even though the process may have started twelve to eighteen months earlier.

Just writing and revising a good proposal can take weeks, even months. The process involves considerable consultation with others and much re-writing. Academic experts at your home institution, leading scholars on the country or topic of interest, and especially host country researchers often provide invaluable feedback on draft proposals. Many scholars also echoed the remarks of one researcher's advocacy of exploratory field visits as a superior way to "meet with as many people as possible relevant to or interested in [your] research in order to garner more insight and suggestions to improve [your] proposal." Diligence and a thick skin are the keys to accepting and profiting from the inevitable and not-always-constructive criticism. That said, there are exceptional cases in which clearly important research topics undertaken by unusually skilled researchers are funded despite an extremely brief proposal-writing period. One contributor, who won a Fulbright grant despite dashing off the application the day after returning from an exploratory trip to the research site, attributes her success to the enthusiasm palpable in her proposal.

The preparation of successful grant proposals is an art in itself. There is no simple recipe to ensure success in the sometimes brutal competition for research funding. Nonetheless, several consistent themes emerge from the scholars we consulted. First, the proposal must offer a clear and concise statement of the question you seek to answer and a strong argument as to why it is important to answer that question. Recognizing that busy people from assorted disciplines read scores of grant applications in the screening process, you should write your proposal in simple, declarative sentences. Attempting to demonstrate the complexity of a problem in a grant pro-posal is likely to prove counterproductive. When possible, directly connect everything that follows the initial thesis statement – theoretical arguments, literature review, discussions of research design and methodology, your qualifications to complete the proposed research – back to the main argument. It sounds simple but is, in fact, very difficult for unpracticed researchers. It is often helpful to look at other proposals, both successful and unsuccessful, as a guide.

Second, identify the interests and objectives of the funding agency, and tailor the proposal accordingly. Most good scholarly research shows promise on more than one level, including theoretical advances, methodological innovations, and contributions to current political debates. Thus, you can emphasize one or another dimension to different prospective donors without misrepresenting yourself. Moreover, this teasing out of different threads in the overall research project is not only useful for winning a grant, but often contributes considerably to the quality of the final research product. But in order to succeed in fundraising, you must know your audience: What are their interests? What have they supported in the past? How much do they usually provide?

Third, one of the most valuable items in a successful grant application for overseas research is a letter of invitation from a host institution, indicating an interest in the proposed research and a willingness to facilitate the project. As mentioned earlier, exploratory visits are a common means by which to secure strong letters from host country institutions and scholars. Unless specifically prohibited, feel free to amend a grant application with supplementary materials, especially letters of recommendation from host country institutions and scholars or research clearances already obtained.

Fourth, be realistic about research design. The broader and more ambitious the project, the more suspicious funding agencies become about its feasibility. For example, visiting multiple countries (unless such multi-country projects are the norm for a particular funding agency, such as the Watson Foundation) introduces the risk that you will encounter serious impediments to a successful research program. You might, for example, run into problems in obtaining all necessary research clearances. Given the difficulties of "settling in" (discussed in Chapter 4), funding agencies might also be concerned about the quality of the fieldwork from a project with multiple and widespread sites. Anyone who has ever fielded a survey appreciates the enormous administrative and logistical challenge of careful data collection across vast spaces and the realities of respondent fatigue. Proposed data collection must not be unrealistically broad in either scope or space.

Fifth, give careful consideration to those asked to write recommendations on behalf of the proposed research and researcher. Not all recommenders carry equal weight with grantsmaking institutions, nor does the relative value of your adviser's words of praise remain constant across donors. But a blind preference for the most prominent scholars carries with it obvious dangers. You need recommenders who can credibly convey an intimate knowledge of the proposed research and abundant confidence in your abilities to complete the project successfully. A mix of some references who are familiar with the project and researcher and those who are well known worked well for many contributors who won major research grants.

It is difficult to advise on the optimal level of specificity in grant proposals. Most people provide reasonably precise identification of a site and timing. Nevertheless, all funding agencies understand that sites and schedules sometimes change (although they might not support dramatic changes). The more ideal your site for the proposed research, the more sense it makes to trumpet this advantage. Just recognize that unforeseen circumstances, such as civil unrest or denial of research clearance, may force you to change sites. If the strength of the grant proposal rests entirely on a single site, which later becomes unfeasible, the funding agency might not approve a revised research design. Thus, some researchers insert "mobility clauses" into grant applications, and most avoid pinning everything on one precisely defined locale.

Most prospective donors require a research project budget. Students routinely cite budgeting as a confusing, frustrating exercise in naive forecasting. For most researchers undertaking their first study in a country, budgeting is a process of gathering scraps of information and making intelligent guesses. The best way to gather the necessary information is through personal observation during an exploratory visit. You might also want to rely on contacts who have done recent research in the site or country, advisers with fieldwork experience, and natives of the research site. Simple web searches provide up-to-date air fares and visa costs. The US State Department posts official travel *per diem* rates for lodging, meals and incidental expenses online and updates them regularly; but be aware that those rates are typically quite high, intended to cover traveling diplomats staying in posh hotels that few students frequent.

Most researchers underestimate the budgetary requirements of their research projects. Some deliberately underestimate the budget under the assumption that asking for "too much" might jeopardize the chances of receiving a grant, although there is little factual basis to support this hypothesis. Moreover, researchers funded on an unnecessarily skimpy budget often live to regret having too little to properly fund data collection, analysis, and basic survival. A special problem often arises for researchers going to economies experiencing high inflation: currency devaluation can throw even a well-researched budget completely out of whack. Those heading to such places need to be especially careful not to underestimate the financial requirements of the project, for funding agencies do not always adjust award levels to account for even severe macroeconomic shocks. Keep in mind as well that changes in exchange rates – which can be dramatic in either direction – can also have an enormous impact on how much money you need. Including a small – typically ten percent – budget line for contingencies is common practice, although not all grantsmaking organizations permit it.

In budgeting, break down expenses by category (international travel, in-country travel, supplies, assistants' compensation, etc.). Do not presume that shortfalls will cancel out across categories. Some donors provide unconditional financing, but other grants' fungibility is sharply limited. For instance, some prohibit surpluses in international travel from being transferred to cover shortfalls in the budget for materials and supplies. Where no set form is provided, many experts at grant writing recommend identifying not just the uses of funds but also the sources. Indicate funding already secured, including any personal savings or borrowing committed to the project. Others' willingness to put money behind the project helps defuse concerns about the value and viability of the proposed research. Whether they expressly acknowledge it or not, most grantsmakers like co-financing.

Researchers who have done their homework, have an interesting subject and appropriate method, and are very lucky sometimes to win multiple grants. It is ethically imperative that you report the full range of grants awarded to each granting agency so as to avoid overlapping funding. At the margin this often permits funding one of an agency's alternate grantees. Even with overlapping contributions eliminated, multiple grants generally yield more generous funding because different agencies pay for different sorts of expenses. Thus one of the co-authors was able to combine four different grants to pay for the considerable expenses involved in fielding a large, formal survey and subsequent analysis.

Moreover, it is often true that money begets money. Receiving a fellowship that pays for a preparatory visit to your research site – or that frees you from other (teaching or research) obligations – often provides the additional insights and time necessary to acquire more substantial funding. Prior funding can also establish you as a "good risk," thereby improving your prospects for receiving funding. So begin the process early.

Be aware that if you are fortunate enough to receive funding, most grantsmaking organizations require some sort of regular reporting, on the technical details of your work, your use of their funding, or both. Find out the reporting requirements and adhere to them precisely. In some cases, funds get routed through one's university or college, which requires receipts for even minute expenses, which requires burdensome, but necessary, bookkeeping. In many developing countries, receipts are unfamiliar, so experienced researchers prepare an all-purpose receipt form that they have pre-cleared with their university's or sponsoring organization's accountants, and then complete receipts as necessary and have the vendor sign. The puzzled looks of illiterate rickshaw drivers as they scribble on a receipt for their transport services offer unusual, treasured memories of fieldwork. The key lesson is to know the requirements, if any, for accounting for funds before you leave and come up with solutions – sometimes creative ones – to satisfy those requirements.

One scholar, herself a recipient of both Fulbright and SSRC dissertation funding, summed up succinctly: "I do not believe that there is any way to 'finesse' the application process. One must simply have a strong, well written and well argued proposal, submit all of the information that they are looking for, and get the application in neatly and on time."

What to do if you do not get (enough) funding? First, and above all, do not lose confidence. The number of qualified applicants in most grants competitions far exceeds the limit of grantsmakers' funds. Sometimes award decisions can appear arbitrary, responding to fashions or the historical prejudices of a particular agency (or, more precisely, of its external reviewers or expert panelists) due to an inability to distinguish among equally meritorious proposals. Every experienced field researcher has been turned down, often frequently. Success one time out of three is uncommonly good.

That said, if funding is not forthcoming for one approach to the project, rethink the proposal, and perhaps reorient it slightly to hook into a larger, preexisting project with available funds. Contact other scholars working in the field, but expect no response; they owe you nothing. Nonetheless, you may be pleasantly surprised at the fruitful advice and opportunities that result from such attempts.

Consider alternative methods of funding your research. Some researchers fund fieldwork (or the extension of a research project begun on a grant) through a professional services contract with a development or conservation agency or with a business. Consulting opportunities abound for researchers in-country with decent academic credentials and good skills and contacts. The crucial consideration regarding such arrangements is whether efforts undertaken under terms of the contract support the original research program sufficiently without compromising academic integrity. Many of our respondents took on related, contractual research that fell outside the scope of their own intended work but could nest their project within it effectively.

Sometimes a project can be broken down into smaller, shorter field stints as funding becomes available piecemeal. Local collaborators can sometimes find inexpensive housing or transport that can reduce costs when one feels a pinch. Housesitting for expatriates away on holiday can likewise help fill holes in a field research budget. Perhaps the most common last ditch approach, especially for students undertaking "action research" with a development project, is to hit upon supportive friends, family and employers for contributions to the cause. This often sparks a desire to keep one's supporters closely connected to the project. Some students blog for this purpose. But, as Kasia Paprocki explains, the self-imposed demands of a blogger doing fieldwork can prove more demanding than one might anticipate.

Box 2.5 To blog or not to blog

I raised money from dozens of small individual donors who became committed to the project and research on a personal level and were thus invested in the success of my work. In order to create an ongoing connection with my project as it proceeded, I committed to keeping a blog during my time overseas to keep them updated on the progress. Before leaving, I understood this to be a sort of simple, public place to record field notes, and to engage the people at home who wanted to understand the work better.

At the beginning, keeping this blog was very simple and straightforward – I documented the place I was living, the people I was meeting, the clothes I was wearing, and posted pictures. The feedback I received from this posting was exciting and rewarding, and kept me enthusiastic about continuing to share my experiences.

However, once I became more engaged with my research, I found this to be an increasingly difficult task to maintain. Besides being a great time drain, I found the commitment to continue sharing stories and having immediate reflections to be more demanding than I expected. When writing field notes, it's possible to reflect on all experiences, both positive and negative, and even to document experiences without immediately knowing their significance. The reflection and insight can come much later, often long after you have left the field. However, maintaining a blog, particularly for donors who have a personal and financial investment in your work, requires a certain feeling of obligation to understanding the significance of the experiences you are having. It also creates a feeling of pressure for success at every step, making it much more difficult when you hit a roadblock or when you don't quite understand something you have learned or experienced. I would recommend that anyone considering keeping a blog while conducting overseas research keeps their expectations low for themselves as far as serious reflection in their writing is concerned, as this can be a much longer process than expected.

Kasia Paprocki

Loans are generally available, either explicitly through a financial institution, friend or relative, or implicitly through credit card use. But loans can be dangerous if they tempt you to skimp on necessary research expenses. Also, if debt servicing induces excessive moonlighting or premature acceptance of permanent employment, borrowing may ultimately degrade the quality of your work. On the other hand, concerns about finishing up before you need to start repaying a debt can also fuel uncommon industriousness, at least according to one scholar who resorted to this method. When absolutely necessary, borrowing appears best left to the write-up stage of a research project, where the risks of cutting corners in data collection are lowest and the need to motivate analysis is sometimes highest.

Finally, you can always search for a pre-existing research project on your chosen topic or in your preferred site. It can be tough to crack the lineup of an established effort, but such opportunities do arise. One good way to start such a search is to contact the operations officers at large donor organizations (e.g. USAID, World Bank) to find out which institutions or individuals have large contracts in force in your area of interest.

Summary

The early stages of defining and funding an overseas research project take a great deal of time and energy. Although most of us hunger to get on with the "real research" and to finish with the annoying administrative, logistical, and emotional preliminaries, researchers consistently advise taking your time in these initial stages. If you rush through site selection and the search for sufficient funding, it will come back to haunt you. Perhaps the most useful advice from the scholars we consulted is not to become impatient or dismayed by delays, changes of plans, or rejections. Consider them not just as the price of progress, but also practice for the field. Patience and perseverance are crucial all along the way, both at home and in the field.

3 Predeparture preparations

Once decided on the site and with funding secured, you still have countless things to attend to before leaving home. In this chapter we suggest some of the issues you need to consider before heading overseas, including many things you might not imagine necessary at first glance. The list ranges from the obvious to the obscure, and we suggest different strategies for approaching the inevitable obstacles of life overseas. We focus on both life's essentials (health, money, family, housing) and academic essentials (contacts, research clearance). Not everything can be done before departure, but there is truth to the adage that "preparation prevents poor performance."

We offer one blanket recommendation: Consult with anyone you possibly can who has recently been to the site in which you will be doing research. They can advise on where you might live, whom you might contact, and other site-specific information. For general information on local conditions, there are of course many internet resources; it is often useful to consult the tourism website of the country where you will be doing research, as this can contain many useful links in a variety of areas. Basic guidebooks (such as *Lonely Planet* or the *Rough Guides*) are also good places to start. Overall, though, the message would be to get to know the site as well as you can before you go.

Money and travel

Practically speaking, issues of money are primary. If you mishandle money, the entire research trip can be disastrous. Much depends on the state of financial technology in the host country, though accessing money in a US bank account is increasingly easy. As one researcher noted, "at least major cities, almost anywhere you go, will have ATMs of one or two international banks." It is important to note, as well, that many ATMs will only work with local bank cards, and you may have to spend some time finding those ATMs that will accept international cards (they usually display the PLUS or Cirrus logo). You may also want to consider setting up a bank account with an international bank that has branches in your host country, as that may allow you better access to your funds from abroad. Keep in mind, however, that many countries have restrictive foreign exchange regulations, and just because the bank has the same name abroad, it will not automatically allow you access to your funds. If you do go down this route, you will want to investigate local financial regulations first.

Put your financial affairs in order before leaving. Bills will have to be paid while you are gone. Depending on the length of one's time abroad, one may want to ensure that such obligations are covered by giving a relative or a trustworthy friend formal power of attorney before leaving. You might leave some signed checks with a trusted friend or family member to carry out financial transactions, as well. Although many rely on family or friends to handle financial matters, it is also relatively easy to pay most bills online, which is often the simplest approach if – and that's a big if – you will have a stable and secure internet connection. Transmitting banking or credit card details on unsecured internet connections is always a bad idea. Regardless of whether or not you use its online banking services, contacts at your home bank can be helpful, especially if problems arise later. Finally, consultation with a lawyer may be necessary for matters more complex than merely paying bills.

Keep in mind that the initial costs of settling in to the field can be substantial, especially if you are going to be abroad for an extended period of time and need to incur significant expenses for a vehicle or other equipment. Expect to incur some debt at the outset of the project if your personal resources are limited. Some researchers rely on loans from parents or relatives, while others take on student loans or more expensive debt, such as credit cards (please note: we strongly caution against expensive credit card debt!). Whatever the financing, it is often necessary to plan to spend more money initially than a grant's first payments provide. Most researchers will agree that going into limited initial debt – as long as one has a realistic plan to get out of it before too long – is worthwhile when launching a research project.

Get and carry a credit card that offers field services, not just financing. Some cards grant holders access to mail services while abroad, or permit you to write checks on a home bank account to receive traveler's checks. Fast and reliable international replacement of a lost or stolen credit card is necessary. The utility of such a service clearly depends on your access to the card issuer's offices. These tend to be confined to cities, so researchers in remote areas might find a credit card of little use. But where an American Express office is accessible, it is highly advisable to have a card. One researcher illustrated the benefits of an American Express card as follows: "I was robbed on a bus in Buenos Aires. I was getting off the bus when I felt a push. After I got off the bus I realized that my wallet was gone. I immediately went home to cancel my credit cards. After phoning about half a dozen telephone numbers, I was finally able to report the theft of my card. The operator told me to report to the Amex office on the next day, and my new Gold Card would be waiting." Other credit card companies offer similar services, and it is wise to check before leaving home.

Credit cards are not always advisable, of course, especially when doing research in rural areas or in countries with a high inflation rate. One of the co-authors encountered a striking reluctance on the part of merchants to accept credit cards (and found that the use of credit cards greatly increased prices) when inflation rates were high, since merchants received payments from banks well after the purchase was made, reducing the real value of their sale. Nevertheless, when they can be used, credit cards often provide a superior (interbank) exchange rate, depending on the local currency regulations and your credit card issuer's fees for currency exchange. Investigate such matters before going to the field. Finally, you will want to call your credit card issuers before you go abroad to explain that you will be using your credit cards regularly while overseas; fraud detection protocols might otherwise flag your card use as fraudulent, and freeze the use of your card(s). Keep in mind that it might take several phone calls to have this resolved; one of the co-authors had to call his card company four times (after they had frozen his card four times) before they made the appropriate notation to his account that he was in fact abroad for an extended period of time, and that use of his card in that venue was legitimate.

Traveler's checks are another option, though less essential and convenient than they used to be. Often, traveler's checks can only be exchanged at official foreign exchange offices, and these are sometimes confined to banks and airports. So, like credit cards, traveler's checks may not work well outside of major urban centers since formal financial networks are often either scarce or absent in the hinterland.

Carrying cash is always a risky option, but a necessary one in some places. When carrying cash, investigate whether exchanging large or small bills is easier, and note that clean and crisp bills are sometimes easier to exchange than older-looking currency. Be careful to note when the local central bank changes the currency, which typically involves replacing older notes worth little with newer ones worth one hundred, one thousand or more times the previous currency. Because the old notes circulate for some time after the official change, foreigners are often vulnerable to scams from street money exchangers who discreetly substitute old, worthless bills for newer ones.

Look into the possibility of setting up a bank account in the host country. Its practicality will depend on local banking regulations, but access to a local account can alleviate the need to carry cash or traveler's checks and minimize the time it takes to deal with the local financial system. Banks are also the safest – if sometimes the most expensive – places in which to exchange foreign currency for local money.

In deciding how to get to the research site, it is easier than ever before to shop around for good airfares. That said, if you are going to be traveling to an out-of-the-way place, most of the common travel search engines used to find flights (such as Expedia or Orbitz) are often less than helpful. Among the best sites for international student fares at the time of writing (July 2009) were kayak.com, statravel.com, and studentuniverse.com. That said, one researcher pointed out that low-cost student tickets are usually quite inflexible, a problem if you need to change flight schedules due to an emergency, delayed research clearance, or other problems. It is also advisable to invest in travel insurance for essential luggage and research materials. Once you relinquish your apartment or house in the United States, renter's insurance generally no longer covers your possessions. A parent's homeowner's or renter's insurance likewise may not cover losses you might suffer. Check on insurance before you leave and make sure anything you cannot afford to lose and replace on your own is covered by a policy and that you know how to file a claim in the event of loss.

Health

There is nothing worse than being caught unprepared for an illness or an emergency. Although you cannot anticipate everything, some general guidelines can help in planning for a relatively healthy time abroad and, should things go wrong, for emergencies.

First, establish what immunization shots you need before going to the field. Your home health provider should be able to identify necessary immunizations for any given site at any given time. The US Centers for Disease Control in Atlanta update this information regularly (www.cdc.gov) as is needed for virtually every location in the world. Another useful source of advice is the International Association for Medical Assistance to Travelers (http://www.iamat.org/), which provides up-to-date information on good hospitals in foreign countries, disease prevalence, and inoculations. You can also consult host country consulate websites to find out which immunizations are needed for entry. The US State Department website usually posts this same information and it is useful to cross-check these sources to make sure you have met all requirements. You absolutely do not want to have to receive an immunization from health officials at your port of entry. And begin this process earlier rather than later, since some immunizations (e.g. hepatitis A and B) require a sequence of shots spaced out over several months.

It is also worth consulting health specialists familiar with the research site regarding the best way to sterilize food and water. In many places, for instance, it is necessary to soak vegetables and fruits in chlorinated water before cooking and eating them. In some places filtration systems work well, while in others chemical sterilization is more effective. Boiling water, while almost always the best way to sterilize water, takes a lot of time and cooking fuel, both of which may be scarce.

More generally, it is highly desirable to be in good physical and mental shape prior to departure. A new environment and diet, exposure to foreign vectors, such as mosquitoes or ticks, and the stress of launching a major research initiative can take a toll on your health, especially on an immune system weakened by inactivity, jet lag, stress, or fatigue.

Nonetheless, most field researchers fall ill no matter how well they prepare themselves. So plan accordingly, taking a good first-aid kit, including syringes if the sterility of the blood supply and even basic medical equipment are questionable. Your physician can write prescriptions for anything – such as syringes – that might raise customs agents' eyebrows. You might also want to consider purchasing a copy of David Werner's *Where There is No Doctor*, which may be the most widely used health manual in the world. As the name suggests, this book can come in handy in emergencies, but is also a good reference for more common ailments. In addition, one scholar offered the following sensible advice:

> My policy is to play it safe, and I have never had more than a slight stomach upset while doing fieldwork in Africa. Even after living in Africa over fifteen years, I do not eat "street food" no matter how good it smells and regardless of how much I want to identify with the informal sector. I am careful about eating uncooked vegetables in restaurants. I drink soda or tea when I am not sure whether the water was boiled. I use a mosquito net. . . . and I am not a hypochondriac!

You also need to think about health insurance. If your grant includes it, make sure that the provided insurance covers all of your needs. It is much less likely that a spouse's or a child's health insurance (much less an unmarried partner's) will be provided; thus, you may need to purchase supplemental insurance. Insurance can be expensive, so financial planning (and grant budgeting) should take such costs into account. Grantsmaking organizations and international programs offices can usually recommend insurance providers, but it pays to compare plans. Furthermore, one researcher made a point of recommending that you should know in advance *exactly* how to file a claim; insurance companies in the United States are notoriously effective at denying claims. Companies that specialize in international coverage – such as HTH Worldwide and CISI – are often a much better bet when it comes to health insurance abroad.

In addition to general health insurance, consider the possibility of potential disasters. This is particularly important for those who will be far away from high-quality medical care and therefore might need rapid medical evacuation. Under such circumstances, think seriously about purchasing evacuation insurance, such as that provided by International SOS. Some of the insurance companies noted above also provide evacuation and repatriation insurance, and the International Student Identity Card (ISIC) also includes medevac and repatriation insurance. You do not want to be caught with a serious injury or illness without the possibility of getting yourself to a place where the best medical care would be available. Furthermore (without meaning to sound alarmist), one researcher who worked in Africa noted that "one or one's family might want to take out a life insurance policy on the researcher (my mother did!!!). Sounds very grim – but there are considerable expenses involved in bringing a body back from overseas and if [such funds] might not be readily or easily available, then a life insurance policy payment might help." Medical evacuation insurance policies usually contain a repatriation rider to cover this contingency. Embassies (individually or as a multinational co-op) often maintain a blood bank in areas where the sterility of hospitals and the screening of the local blood supply are poor. It is thus worth checking out whether you can participate in such a plan, as insurance and for peace of mind in the event of an accident or emergency surgery. Finally, make sure you know where the nearest (and also the best) hospital is in your research site.

You can prepare for common illnesses. First, establish which diseases are endemic to the region(s) and season(s) of your research. If malaria is widespread, find out whether local strains are chloroquine resistant and know the recommended preventive and curative measures. When working in a malarial area, take along a mosquito net, especially the tent-type that fully seals a sleeping area. Insect repellent or smoke coils often help keep mosquitoes away. Finally, given the AIDS epidemic, proper protection and precautions regarding transmission of the HIV virus and other sexually transmitted diseases are absolutely essential.

Intestinal problems are common for many overseas researchers, often due to parasites picked up from contaminated water. One researcher warned that "the worst thing you can do in that case is take an over-the-counter diarrhea medicine like Pepto Bismol or Maalox. These medicines act like corks, and they just stop you up, allowing the parasite to go on living and reproducing thousands of times in your system." Depending on the nature of the illness, an antibiotic may be necessary, though be wary of self-diagnosis. As one scholar advised, "If the illness is serious enough to consider taking something, then it [is] serious enough to consult a doctor. . . . Regardless of the state of local medical facilities, local doctors are likely to know more about illnesses in the area than someone who has only recently arrived."

Heidi Gjerstsen notes how health issues can both trip up and give greater perspective to a research project.

Box 3.1 Fever

Contracting dengue fever in the Philippines halfway through my first fieldwork experience was a terrifying situation. After a nauseating overnight ride on the floor of a boat to get to a hospital, I arrived in a feverish state only to hear that I needed to begin looking for blood donors in case I required a blood transfusion! This potential procedure became a daily worry, even as the physical discomfort began subsiding. Added to the fact that I had been in the field for three months and still had 20 sites to visit, it was overwhelming to consider continuing my work and risking another illness. Fortunately, my adviser reassured me that I didn't need to think about getting back to work and just to focus on my health. When I recovered, I decided to return with my assistants to the field, but to improve the comfort of our working conditions and efficiency of our routine. This included dropping the remaining sites in the area where I had been infected, living in one town for longer periods of time and hiring a vehicle to bring us to our sites, and taking all possible precautions against mosquito bites! Fortunately, the second half of our research was much easier. Whether we had become closer as a result of the dengue incident or were finally seeing an end to the grueling fieldwork, our spirits were noticeably lighter as we enjoyed the areas we visited and the people we met.

Heidi Gjerstsen

Another set of health issues confronts those with preexisting medical conditions, who may need to bring large amounts of prescription medications. In regions where drug trafficking is common, you may be asked to open bottles or to show a prescription. So be prepared with a letter from your doctor stating your condition and special needs. This can help with both government and medical authorities. Some prescription medicines may not be legal in the country where you will be doing research; in such cases, you should consult your doctor well before your time abroad to see if there are alternative treatments and what regulations your host country might have for importing medicines for personal use.

Keep in mind that if you are going to need research assistants, it is your responsibility to provide for their health care as well. As one economist who utilized several research assistants put it, "I don't think anyone on the project should feel less well protected than another." Given the privileged position in which most western researchers find themselves, this seems a sound principle.

Having your children in the field presents special health concerns, since they tend to be more susceptible to illnesses and need more frequent preventive and curative care. The above recommendations also apply to children, although you need to pay special attention to vaccinations and malaria prophylaxis, some of which are too powerful for small children. Consult with a pediatrician well in advance of taking young children overseas. As most researchers who have gone abroad with their children will attest, responsibility for children generally heightens parents' sensitivity to health-related issues. Ironically, often, the care given to children's health is not always extended to oneself. One researcher commented that he and his wife "would have been well-advised to consistently follow the same precautions" they did for their child.

When accompanied to the field by a child, consult with your pediatrician in advance about any special precautions that should be taken in advance of travel. And identify a pediatrician as soon as you arrive on site, if not before. One researcher noted that an effective way to find a pediatrician is to consult with local day-care providers. Local academic contacts and recommendations from the expatriate community also often prove helpful. Take your children's medical records with you, including the yellow, international standard vaccination booklet issued and approved by the World Health Organization, with all their vaccinations duly inscribed.

We also recommend that if you take your children with you, you have a notarized letter from each parent authorizing that either parent may travel alone with the child if necessary and that the child may travel alone in case of emergency. Your children will also need their own passports and visas. Allow months to obtain those; seriously.

Housing

The key to finding satisfactory housing is simple to articulate but difficult to execute: you have to be happy where you are living. There is nothing worse than coming home from a difficult day of dealing with bureaucrats or interviewing farmers or a fruitless day in the archives to a place that you find uncomfortable, dangerous or depressing. The trick is to find a place you deem acceptable financially and psychologically.

Looking for housing takes a lot of time, either before going to the field, upon arriving, or both. We discuss the search for a dwelling after your arrival on site in the next chapter; here we focus briefly on what you can do before leaving.

In an ideal world, you would settle housing arrangements before leaving. Usually, this proves impossible; most researchers find a place to live after they arrive. Those who reported success in lining up housing prior to arrival were able to do so because of local contacts established earlier. Most such contacts were typically made on previous research trips. It is obviously much easier to set up housing before arrival if you are familiar with the layout of the city or village.

More frequently, however, the most you can do from home is arrange for temporary accommodations for the days or weeks immediately following arrival. This is probably safer, in any event, if you have not seen the apartment or house on offer. The expatriate community often has embassy guest houses or knows of a family on extended vacation that would welcome a housesitter, so early contact with embassy contacts can be fruitful. You might also be able to arrange to stay with friends at the research site, which can serve as a base from which to look for more permanent lodging. One researcher also suggested church guest houses; another suggested NGO guest houses. These arrangements can provide a homely atmosphere and useful contacts. In any of these arrangements, you should be careful not to overstay your welcome.

The most common short-term lodging preparation is to reserve a hotel room for your date of arrival. If the hotel arrangements are unsatisfactory, you can always change hotels. One researcher's experience shows several sides of the option:

> In a desperate move to have some illusion of security and "home" in the field, I reserved an apartment in a hotel in the downtown area before I left. . . . This turned out to be financially costly, psychically isolating, and damaging to my reputation. Being a woman staying in a hotel notorious for being a place where expatriates find Kenyan lovers did not help my attempts to be professional and above reproach. Nonetheless, reserving the hotel room did give me some peace of mind for the period during which I was preparing to leave the States and traveling to Kenya . . . and gave me a base from which to locate alternative housing, which I eventually did.

In the next chapter we will discuss in more detail some of the important issues involved in looking for a more permanent abode.

Packing: what to bring, what to leave

Most researchers report that they mispacked when they went to the field, either bringing unnecessary items or forgetting absolutely essential (though easily overlooked) ones. There are no general rules here, and much depends on where and when you are going, and your personal preferences. Again, an exploratory research visit can clarify the issue. In this section we simply list what researchers have reported as "essentials" they forgot and "non-essentials" that weighed down their bags and took up space. Not all will be relevant to everyone, but the listing should provide a starting point. Research equipment and ancillary tools are addressed separately in Chapter 5.

Do not forget:
- **Business cards**. In urban areas in particular, business cards can prove essential. Information on it should include: name, address, phone, fax and email, as well as your affiliation and title. Introduce yourself with a card and expect to receive one in return. It is a serious professional *faux pas* in many cultures not to have a card. For whatever reason, having cards adds an air of seriousness to your endeavor. If you can get them embossed with your home institution's seal, all the better. The more that one is dealing with elites in one's research, the more necessary are business cards. One researcher also notes that you should be careful about what you put on your business card: "it probably makes sense not to include a cell phone number on these cards, and handwrite the cell number onto cards being given to someone you really trust. I definitely regretted giving my cell phone number to certain people who would not stop calling . . ."

- **Toiletries.** What is needed obviously depends on what is available in-country. You will want to consult with those who have been to the research site recently. What you bring will also depend on what you consider "essential," and how much change of routine you can handle without getting frustrated. Recognize that even in countries where the same brands as at home can be found, they are often much more expensive overseas, sometimes by a factor of two or three. For this reason, some experienced researchers recommend bringing a reasonable supply of the following items: shampoo, hair conditioner, deodorant, sunscreen, insect repellent, tampons, vitamin supplements, towelettes or moist hand wipes, contact lens paraphernalia, and skin moisturizer.
- **Extra eyeglasses or contact lenses.** These are often difficult or expensive to replace, so take at least one extra pair. Be sure to bring your eyeglass and contact lens prescriptions as well.
- **Travel iron.** This can prove invaluable if you expect to travel a lot and need to maintain a respectable appearance.
- **Birth control.** Many researchers report that finding any manner of birth control is difficult. Some also report that even where they are available, the quality of condoms sold in some countries is questionable. Enough said.
- **Gifts.** These can often be simple and lightweight, but it is good to show up with something to give many people with whom you will come into contact while in the field. As Daniel Aldrich (2009: 301) noted, "In my own case, before departing for the field I stopped by the bookstore to pick up handfuls of Harvard lapel pins. While inexpensive, they displayed my home institution and also worked as a way to break the ice with informants." The local dollar store is a great resource for simple, inexpensive, practical gifts that are easy to transport and much appreciated by many people with whom you will interact, especially in poorer and remote areas. Simple toys to occupy village kids are often a good way to build rapport and to keep the children occupied while you speak with the adults about your research.
- **A local language/English dictionary.** This is something most researchers find essential, unless they are truly fluent in the language of the host country.
- **An International Student Identity Card.** Depending on location, an ISIC card comes in handy when purchasing discounted air tickets, obtaining reduced admission to museums, etc. It also provides medevac/repatriation insurance.
- **A flashlight.** This is especially crucial in areas subject to frequent blackouts, or in places where access to electricity is limited. Do not forget a spare bulb; these can be excruciatingly difficult to find overseas. Headlamps might also be a good option. One researcher noted that you should get "one of those wind-up, rechargeable flashlights. They seem pretty gimmicky on the shelf at REI, but everyone we met abroad wished they had one just like ours."

- **Pepper spray**. One researcher noted that "it is a good item for any woman to carry. I always had mine in my bag and there were a couple of times that I almost had to use it and was relieved that it was there."
- **Electrical adapters and surge suppressors**. Find out the kind of outlet(s) the country uses, as well as the voltage typically available (it may be different in rural and urban areas of the same country) to see if an adapter is necessary. And ask around to see how reliable the electricity supply is. Power surges can fry expensive electronics in an instant. Bring adequate, good quality surge suppressors to protect all your valuable electronics. Keep in mind, too, that if you connect your computer directly to telephone lines via a dial-up modem, lightning strikes on telephone poles can cause massive damage. Your local electronics store should have telephone surge suppressors – or joint power and telephone units – available if this pattern of use applies to you.
- **Rechargeable batteries and battery charger**. These can come in handy and, in addition to being environmentally responsible, can save a substantial amount of money when using electronics to record interviews or play music.
- **Children's possessions**. One researcher reported that, "especially with small kids, it was absolutely necessary to take along . . . toys, blankets, books, etc. . . . Nothing fouls up great research plans quicker than distraught kids, and the dislocation of a new house, new school, no friends and a strange place can be quite unsettling to kids of a certain age. We took along more than I thought was necessary at the time, but it turned out to be the bare minimum. It is worth excess baggage [charges] to soften the impact of displacement on young kids." In a related vein, another researcher noted that one of the best things that he and his wife brought along to the field was a book on child development and health care, which gave them great peace of mind.
- **Shortwave radio**. Where the local press is heavily censored or in remote areas, a shortwave radio can be a valuable link to the outside world. It can also be a useful research tool for tracking the local reporting of domestic and international events and the international reporting of local events.
- **Office supplies**. Bring from home such things as academic department letterhead, and Post-It notes, which can be hard to come by (or are very expensive) in the research site.
- **Small electronics**. Most obviously, bring a few extra USB flash drives. They are cheap and invaluable for backing up and transferring data. A digital voice recorder often comes in handy, either for doing interviews or recording your own thoughts. If you plan to record interviews, be sure to get a good quality microphone so that you don't lose essential information due to poor audio quality on the recording. A decent quality, compact digital camera is likewise invaluable, both for taking photos of your research site(s) to spruce up presentations and to be able

to send photos back to friends and family. Plus, printed photos are almost always a welcome thank you gift to informants and assistants in the field. But be careful not to take more electronic gadgetry than you need, nor more expensive items than you can afford to replace if they get broken or stolen.

- **Pleasure reading and music.** A few novels or other books completely unconnected to one's own work will be a welcome diversion from research, from which distraction is often necessary. Likewise, music is often a soothing balm after a noisy, stressful day in an unfamiliar place. A simple player and headphones or compact speakers provide a wonderful escape when you need it.

- **A first-aid kit.** There will be ample opportunity to use it, for others as well as for yourself. Keep it small and lightweight, though it is well worth the baggage space.

- **A portable scanner.** There are pen-sized scanners available now, and for those who need to have a record of the documents they encounter, being able to have electronic versions available can be invaluable (and can significantly reduce the burden of bringing hard copies of materials back home).

Lest you feel we are only adding to the burden of packing, experienced scholars consistently offered the following two recommendations on what could safely be left at home, usually without serious consequences:

- **Academic books and other academic materials.** Many researchers lamented having brought so much of their "essential" work materials with them. Academic books and files of articles are, of course, nice to have for handy reference (and taking a *few* is sensible). There will be times when you wish you had everything you've ever read along, but the truth of it is, most of your time will be spent exploring and tracking new information rather than perusing old materials. Certainly, while in the field, you will be attempting to fit this new information into frameworks, ideas, and theories contained in your personal library, but it is rarely necessary to have these physically at hand. As one researcher noted,

> I did send along about twenty-five books in advance of my arrival. My adviser tried to dissuade me [from] this, and ultimately I believe that he was right. These were core books in my field that I thought I would have time to read or that I might need in the event of having to make a presentation, etc. I may have read a few but never used any for a presentation. I would strongly advise against bringing any or many books into the field; they only become a nuisance as one moves around and even more so when it comes time to leave the field. They will almost certainly not be read or used. One will have all one can do to read the new material gathered in the field.

Since there will almost certainly be plenty of heavy materials in the form of newly acquired books, photocopies, other field data, and surveys to bring back, you won't want to add to your burden. Furthermore, you should be able to bring much important information along with you in electronic form, as pdf files, for example. When bringing such materials along, you should also back them up, including one set of copies on your laptop and another on a USB pen drive that you store separately from your computer. Many experienced researchers establish a restricted-access web download or FTP site, with automated backup, at their home university so they can access materials remotely in the event of a catastrophic loss of hardware or files.

- **Clothing**. Many researchers pack an unmanageably large wardrobe for fieldwork. In particular, articles requiring special care (e.g. dry cleaning) often prove expensive to maintain and are worn infrequently. Clothes take a beating in rudimentary laundering and in the wear and tear of rugged areas, so do not take articles you cannot bear to see ripped, faded, or otherwise damaged. Moreover, you can purchase clothing overseas, usually quite cheaply. Although sometimes of mediocre quality, the clothing available locally is often better suited to the climate than that available at home. Nevertheless, a caveat is in order: you need to pay attention to appearance, and we (and a number of our contributors) suggest you make a serious effort to adapt to local sensibilities, which may include jacket and tie for men and skirts or dresses for women, as Aili Tripp points out.

Box 3.2 Dressing the part in the field

Depending on the topic and the person being interviewed, it may be necessary to maintain a more "professional" appearance than what is acceptable or desirable among grad students studying in the United States. One need not go broke or have an extensive wardrobe, but in many cultures an excessively casual appearance (e.g. jeans, T shirts, cutoffs) may have some negative consequences for one's research. Dressing in an overly casual manner may imply you do not respect yourself or that you do not respect the people with whom you are coming into contact. It may also suggest that you are not dressing according to your status and therefore are showing disrespect [to the interviewee], and it may reveal a certain amount of immaturity. In addition, it may give the impression that you are younger than you are. Where we may think that dressing nicely may be a sign of being pretentious and a way of accentuating class differences, others in the country of study, even in rural areas, may think that by not dressing "properly," especially when we could afford to, we are showing a certain amount of disrespect and carelessness. For women in countries with large Muslim populations and in most African countries, shorts, long pants, and short skirts are considered clothes of prostitutes and loose women. Often people excuse it in a foreigner because they chalk it up to ignorance, but it still indicates a lack of awareness of the values of the culture one is working in.

Aili Tripp

Family matters

For those with families (broadly defined), a crucial decision concerns whether to take them to the field. In an ideal world, one would almost always want to take loved ones along, but in reality many obstacles stand in the way. Considerations in making this decision include, among other things, a spouse/partner's career and potential work opportunities at home and abroad, the length of time away from home, the amount of travel to expect while in the field, the potential threats to the family's health and safety, and the additional expense of having the family with you. If there are children, there is also the matter of schooling or day care. The adjustment costs (including time) of settling a family generally preclude bringing them along on short research trips. But the emotional toll of extended separation makes it difficult to leave them at home for longer durations.

Choosing to leave the family at home almost inevitably increases the stress felt by both the researcher and the family. All miss the daily companionship unique to a long-term relationship or the joys and frustrations of parenthood. The research experience is, after all, an intense one, and most researchers want to share this experience with companions. The inability to do so can be frustrating, even debilitating. One researcher who was away for six months during one stretch and ten in another found it too taxing alone: "I, like most people who decide to do international research, am an independent kind of person. This does not mean, though, that living alone in a foreign country is easy [for me] . . . I don't think I want to live alone overseas for this length of time again." Indeed, long stretches without a partner can be especially taxing. Visits from the family may need to be planned. When family does visit, another researcher advised taking "some time off work. . . . It might be interesting for them to see you at work for a while, but, especially if they don't speak the local language, they might eventually feel neglected."

If the family stays behind, make appropriate arrangements for them before leaving, especially if there are children. With children at home, a support group for the remaining spouse is absolutely essential. The absence of one parent seriously upsets family life, and everything possible should be done to alleviate the substantial burden on the parent remaining at home. Arranging extraordinary day care, helpful visitors, or a cleaning service can help to compensate. Regular contact can be managed in a number of economical ways, including the use of regular email and video Skype conversations, as well as more conventional cell phone calls and letters.

There are, of course, plenty of good reasons to take your family to the field (and if they do travel with you, be sure to bring along birth and marriage certificates). As one researcher put it, "my partner and I talked about separating for a year, but I'm glad we didn't. It would have been difficult, I think, to recount the experience that I'd had. Having a partner along not only helps to pass the time, but can be an additional source of information, learning, and experience." On the other hand, the experience can also create problems for the partner. A nearly universal concern is what the partner does with her or his time during the research period. Especially if the partner is used to working or studying outside the home, it is important to put some thought into this. Finding a new routine is often especially difficult for a partner. Having children may alleviate some problems, in that it provides one with extra social opportunities, but as Darren Hawkins's comments make clear, having children along can cut both ways.

Box 3.3 Obstacles to family adjustment in the field

For my wife and child, adjusting to the new culture and language was the most difficult problem we experienced and never successfully resolved. My wife had enjoyed "staying home" and being a mother in the States, but it didn't work out in Santiago [Chile]. Putting our daughter in child care wasn't really an option as she had severe stranger anxiety at the time and my wife wanted to care for her. The problem was that there was not much to do. In the States, my wife could get in the car and go to the children's museum and library, or just run errands. She could also go to [children's] play groups, La Leche League meetings, etc. Few, if any, of these options were available in Santiago. Many mothers did indeed stay at home, but seemed far more interested in cleaning their homes and cooking lunch or dinner ... than [in] getting together [with other mothers] for anything resembling a play group. My wife spoke little Spanish and found it difficult to make friends. The lack of a car made it difficult to get around. Though the bus system is "good," it's difficult to hop on a bus that only comes to a semi-stop with a two-year-old. We did meet some North Americans with kids, but found them to be so wrapped up in their own children's schooling and so well taken care of by the US embassy or multinational corporations that they had little time or interest in us. It was hard for my wife to relate to people who complained about their maids when we were struggling financially and she was experiencing high levels of culture shock. We hired a tutor, which worked out fairly nicely, except that it was also expensive. We made friends with a few neighbors, which did work out very well. But it was a daily struggle for my wife not to be bored silly.

Darren Hawkins

What we sometimes call "non-traditional" family circumstances place special burdens on the researcher, in particular for the lesbian or gay field researcher. One researcher pointed out that in many countries same-sex relationships are illegal, so LGBT researchers should make sure they understand what to do and not to do safely in their research site. A good site for resources discussing LGBT issues is the NAFSA: Association of International Educators' Rainbow SIG website (www.rainbowsig.org). As another researcher explained: "Family commitments are never discussed in formal academic settings in choosing the field site. Nonetheless, families exist, often silently for the lesbian or gay researcher. . . . My experience and that of other student researchers I have observed indicate field research (as well as graduate school) favors the young, the straight, and the economically advantaged." This scholar went on to recommend some steps that the lesbian or gay researcher might take to ease the transition to fieldwork:

> First, investigate and consider thoroughly the homophobia of the community to which you will relocate. . . . There may be a city or, more likely, a sector of a city reasonably close to your field site that is more tolerant of queers or is known for its queer community. Exploratory research will be mandatory. Take your partner along. If things don't turn out well, you can always cut it short. It's much easier to regroup from a bad exploratory research experience than to find out your site is unworkable during a more extensive period in the field. This is a worst case scenario, however. One can imagine many ways to accommodate both a partner and safety. The arrangements will depend, in part, on the particular field site, the local customs and cultural values toward lesbians and gays, and men living together or being seen together often, which can be very different from the attitudes toward women living together or being seen together often.

This reinforces the advice presented in Chapter 2: Make an exploratory research trip if at all possible.

Finally, if you take your family to a place where gender roles and customs are drastically different from those to which you are accustomed, your family must be prepared. One male researcher who had his family with him for two months in a Muslim society noted that:

Very little English is spoken in Yemen, so my family was very dependent on me. Strict separation of the genders in Yemen also created difficulties for my wife; she could be with women but there was no translation. This made life difficult for her and I spent a lot of time entertaining the family. Fortunately their visit coincided with the month of Ramadan, when very little work could have been done in any case. On the other hand, the presence of my family facilitated my integration into the local community of my research site. The lone male (especially a foreigner) is perceived as socially dangerous, and the presence of my family seemed to relieve my neighbors.

It clearly makes sense to consider how cultural differences in gender roles might affect your research and happiness in the field before the fieldwork begins.

Lest it appear that we are pointing only to the problems associated with bringing the family to the field, we should emphasize that aside from the obvious emotional benefits of having your spouse and children in the field, the family can help the researcher in practical aspects of research. For example, one of the co-authors benefited greatly from his wife's willingness to help in the research process by making telephone calls to set up interviews (often a time-consuming process) and collecting research materials from libraries. Another researcher found, much to his surprise, that his children's playmates helped him make important contacts through their parents or grandparents. Although obviously idiosyncratic, such accidents are probably more common than is typically assumed.

Academic preparations

Up to this point we have been concerned with personal matters in preparation for the work in the field. While these issues are important, the primary task is clearly the actual research project. The final section of the chapter focuses on preparations for work.

The most general piece of advice offered by experienced fieldworkers is to contact as many researchers familiar with the site or subject as possible before going to the field. Contacts at your home institution (and elsewhere) can usually help in this regard, but do not be reluctant to make "cold" calls or write emails to experienced researchers to whom you have no third-party introduction. As one contributor pointed out,

When I think of the useful advice to give someone leaving to conduct research in West Africa, I would emphasize the importance of developing contacts before departing. A means to begin is to contact scholars in the United States who have worked in that country. The Africanist community is not terribly large, and most people are pleased to help someone with names and addresses. Then, mailing follow-up notes will help establish cordial relations before arriving in the country. Such contacts are extremely important for conducting research and the people should be respected and included in any acknowledgments and on the mailing lists for subsequent publications.

Such advice is obviously not limited only to Africanists. Most research communities are relatively small, and many people in them are willing to help if asked, and should be acknowledged if they do.

At the same time you may encounter reluctance from veteran researchers for any of a variety of reasons. The veteran may find the intellectual project of a new researcher suspect. Or the experienced scholar may be reluctant to reveal names of sensitive contacts without first getting to know you and your project in more detail. This natural (and sensible) resistance should not be taken personally, nor is it necessarily a sign that the veteran researcher is not willing to help. As one researcher who has been asked for contacts put it, "I do agree that people should seek out contacts in the US who can help them, but they shouldn't have unrealistic expectations."

In the process of preparing academically, it is usually useful to establish contacts with a local research institution or university, as we discussed in Chapter 2. Such contacts can facilitate access to libraries, local academics and their contacts, photocopying facilities, and secretarial assistance. An institutional affiliation can also help you establish electronic communications, including internet access. Furthermore, such affiliations can often provide potential research assistants or enumerators, many of whom have invaluable research experience. Often the first step in arranging an affiliation is a formal, written request for support. One researcher recommends "securing an official letter of introduction (in a local language) from the president/chancellor of the home institution. In many parts of the world, nothing works better than official letterhead to assuage the obstructionist tendencies of a customs, government, or academic official."

Affiliations are not always what one hopes for, however. An institution's resources and personnel determine the value of affiliation to the researcher, as one pointed out: "I wrote a letter, cold, to an institution in Costa Rica which was kind enough to write back. But once I got there, they really only did two useful things for me: write me letters to help me renew my visa every three months, and give me a connection which helped with a very difficult situation getting government data. These are no small things. They weren't what I expected but I sure did need them." You should have realistic, even if limited, expectations of what a local research institute can do, which is often a consequence of the limited resources that research institutes in many developing countries face. And as another researcher pointed out, making mutual expectations clear can help greatly:

Of all the work that a researcher could do at home to prepare for traveling overseas, I would say that putting in some time to establish shared expectations with a partner organization could be the most helpful to you later on. I would have saved myself a lot of stress and frustration if I had made my boundaries clear from the very beginning, and if I would have asked directly from the start what obligations they imagined on my part (time, financial, etc.). "No, I will not pay for overhead and staff salaries out of my research budget," "No, I will not teach six English classes a week on top of the rest of my workload." If we had been on the same page about these things before I arrived, my research would have gone much smoother (or, I might have found another partner to work with . . .).

How one goes about communicating directly about expectations will of course vary by culture, and you may want to talk to those who have experience in your particular research site for advice on how to approach this potentially sensitive topic.

Another crucial part of the preparation piece is making sure you have read and digested as much as possible about your site and topic before going to the field. You certainly want to show up informed – there is nothing worse than looking or feeling academically unprepared when you are in the field. After all, this was something that you *could* control. As Hertel *et al.* (2009: 305) note, "Read everything on your topic in your library and available through inter-library loan and the internet. You may be surprised to find out how much is there already. Interviews will be most productive, and field research will be most cost-efficient, if scholars collect and digest as much of this as possible prior to entering the field." You will want to use your field time to do things uniquely available in the field, not for things you could have done at home. Think of it this way: you will want to take advantage of the unique time you will have to do research abroad for its own uniqueness. You don't want to spend time doing things in the field that you could do from the comfort of your home.

In addition to making contacts in the field before departure and reading up on your topic, also make arrangements to keep in touch with researchers at home, whether your academic adviser (if you are a student) or colleagues. Cybercafés and wireless hotspots are readily available in many places, and it is often possible to get a cheap international phone card abroad. Bring an inexpensive headset to make cheap or free Skype calls over the internet. While we sometimes lament the degree to which the ease of international communication makes it more difficult to be "away" now, such communication can make an enormous difference to the quality of a research experience and to the final product of that research.

Although some may want to return home during the fieldwork to take a break or check with advisers, this can prove financially onerous if not covered by the basic research grant (or some other patron). If the return home is not easy, then being able to bounce an idea or a change in research focus off other academics or an adviser can prove invaluable. After all, your thinking about academic work tends to change while in the field – usually for the better – and if you are isolated from others who are, in effect, your audience, you can make serious mistakes and waste valuable fieldwork time. When collaborating with other researchers, such contact is all the more vital. Keep in mind also that some grantsmakers will want mid-stream progress reports, so you will need to communicate your progress in any event.

One bit of preparatory advice is especially relevant for undergraduates doing research abroad who may not have quite as extensive methodological training as graduate students do. As one student who conducted research as an undergraduate on Russian Germans during a very short research trip noted,

> One thing that I wish I had done differently was testing the surveys I conducted prior to arriving at my site. My survey was a list of about 30 questions that sought to capture the Russian Germans' subjective feelings about the success of their integration into German society and to assess those subjective results against different factors such as age, sex, level of education, language spoken at home, economic activity, etc. I had translated the survey questions into German and Russian and brought with me a stack of copies. However, I soon discovered that the subjects did not understand some of my questions or failed to give answers that were relevant to my study. I therefore had to amend the surveys on the go and redistribute them to some of the subjects. I wish I had thought of testing the survey on a few of my friends at home before leaving for Germany.

Since undergraduates usually have much less time to prepare and think through research design, and must often conduct research trips on a much tighter timetable, they are generally at a greater risk of having a research trip end up with limited results. Although this researcher ended up with a successful outcome because of an ability to adjust quickly on the fly, he points to a simple thing that could have made his research process much smoother.

Securing research clearances

A foreign researcher often needs research clearance, or at least a research visa, before being allowed into a country. In some countries this can be difficult, especially if the researcher is investigating somewhat sensitive topics. One scholar reported to Social Science Research Council (SSRC) on his return from an exploratory research trip, "I am more acutely aware of the . . . government's sensitivity to the issues I had planned to examine and of the difficulties of carrying out research that is not to the government's liking." It became plain to this individual that his "original research plans would not be feasible without extensive and risky subterfuge," and he subsequently (and appropriately) adjusted the research topic and design. The more authoritarian (or protective of information) the regime in power, the more difficult it may prove to get formal clearance through normal, formal channels. As one researcher who did his work in China noted,

> I really want to stress the difficulties confronting research in oppressed political systems. We tend to assume that we can go abroad and just collect data and conduct interviews. In essence, research is a messy process, especially when politics is involved. I adopted a "Chinese way" of conducting research through individual contacts rather than through the normal bureaucratic routes associated with the Commissions of State Education. This commission has been known to hinder research by denying access to interviewees and research sites. My so-called Chinese way was to rely on contacts to gain inroads into realms not often traveled by foreign researchers.

Informal points of access are often crucial, especially in countries where the formal contacts are meant to place obstacles in the way of the researcher. Nevertheless, to navigate these waters, you should have a very thorough understanding of local politics. This knowledge can be expanded substantially through frequent and early contact with researchers who have been to the research site before.

The need for sensitivity to local politics is pronounced when one needs formal research clearance. As Karen Booth points out in the following narrative, even careful prior consideration of the politics of securing research clearance may miss important issues.

Box 3.4 The complications of research clearance

My process of securing research clearance in Kenya alternated between the hysterical and the banal and ended in anti-climactic success. The Kenyan government is infamous among American Africanist scholars for being exceptionally slow and unenthusiastic about granting research clearance. The process of getting clearance for AIDS research is, on the surface at least, even more difficult; the proposal has to be approved by a committee in the Ministry of Health and then by the President's office. When I told Africans in the know that I not only wanted to study policy in Kenya but that I was interested in prostitutes and AIDS, the modal response was something to the effect of: "you have got to be kidding; go to Uganda." Decidedly daunted but irrationally stubborn, I depoliticized my proposal by replacing all the references to prostitutes with the term women and all the references to sex with reproduction. I then sent it off to a politically savvy Kenyan friend. My friend sent it back saying it was still too controversial. So I depoliticized further by organizing the study around an apparently "technical" policy problem which the World Health Organization had already addressed, which had become part of the discourse in development and health circles in Kenya, and which fit with a mainstream, not inherently revolutionary, concern with "women and development."

This proposal I submitted to the AIDS committee, on the advice that I wait for their approval before allowing the President's office to see my ideas. My first mistake was to ask my friend to deliver the proposal to the committee. This was a *faux pas* on several levels. First, my friend was a peon within the hierarchy of the medical research bureaucracy; his low status reflected on me. Second, my friend was in the political bad graces of the head of the committee; his politics (with which I in fact agreed) made me suspect. Third, my friend was not affiliated with the project with which I requested to work; his role in my research was not clear to the committee – and mattered. In other words, the process or channel of communication was at least as important as the content of the proposal. Unwittingly I had repoliticized at an interpersonal level what I had taken such pains to depoliticize at an intellectual level.

I did not, however, discover that this was a large part of the reason that I had not heard anything on my proposal until I arrived in Kenya on a tourist visa. A number of people in the States had warned me not to go to Kenya without research clearance. My experience is evidence that this is not always the best policy. It was only when I was there, able to find out who really mattered in the committee, hand-deliver my proposal, apologize profusely for my ignorant lack of protocol, and explain the nature of the study that I was able to get my proposal onto the committee's agenda and find a backer for it. This process occupied me for six weeks, during which time I was able to make some invaluable connections, understand the living situation in Nairobi, and have lots of unproductive panic sessions about how I could change my dissertation if I didn't get clearance. I handed over responsibility for the process to my Kenyan adviser and left to do the Geneva portion of my fieldwork, hoping optimistically to return fully cleared in three months.

In Geneva I heard nothing until I ran into my Kenyan adviser at a conference nearly three months later. She said that I would get my clearance in August. August came and I had heard nothing. I wrote to someone in Kenya who discovered that my proposal had not even been discussed by the committee. Enter hysteria. It was, obviously, time for dissertation plan B. I restructured my proposal, experienced an enormous amount of relief as well as regret and self-recrimination at the prospect of not doing the Nairobi fieldwork when I received in the mail in late September a very brief letter: The Committee had approved the proposal and I should come to Nairobi to get the President's rubber stamp. I can't really describe the psychic impact of this turn of events. I had to do a total reversal in a day. I worried that I'd get back and still not get the President's approval and have my hands tied once again. I relived all the anxiety about entering the field and doing ethnography that I should have gotten over months before. And I went back. The first week I was there, I walked into the President's office and was given a research clearance paper after a half-hour wait.

Karen Booth

As Karen Booth demonstrates, many mistakes can occur in the process of "placing" yourself in a research context. Sometimes, the errors emerge from a misplaced or misunderstood sensitivity about what is and what is not acceptable in a particular country. As one researcher recounted, his eventual choice of institutional affiliation was inappropriate:

I chose to establish a formal affiliation with an institution on the mistaken assumption that because of my research topic, which dealt with the business community, an affiliation with a more conservative institution would open more doors. This, I believe, turned out to be a poor criterion for choosing an institutional affiliation and instead I should have made a choice based on what institution would provide the greatest support for my research.

The lesson of this particular experience is not that political factors should not influence your affiliation with a local institution; rather, your assumptions can often be wrong about those factors. Grasping what to do and making the appropriate contact for your particular research topic are not easy tasks, and figuring out the appropriate ways to approach the research task before one goes to the field can help to grease the wheels of research in many ways. Again, the advice to consult with others who have been to your particular "field" before merits reemphasis.

Beyond research clearance from a host government, many universities require students, staff and faculty to secure approval from an Institutional Review Board (IRB) before conducting research on or about "human subjects". The basic principle is simple: do no harm. In an increasingly litigious atmosphere, and following some high-profile ethical lapses in academic research on at-risk peoples, most colleges and universities now have formal procedures for securing approval of any research project that involves observation of, discussion with, or experimentation on people.

While these rules were generally put in place with an eye toward biomedical experiments, the IRB's domain commonly extends into anything involving collecting data of any sort from people, even using data others have collected if it can be readily traced back to individual respondents/participants. Researchers intending to work with human subjects must usually complete a short course on research ethics, typically an online module lasting an hour or so, followed by formal review of a specific research plan by an IRB. Approval requirements vary markedly among institutions. Some require a formal risk assessment, others a copy of one's questionnaire or script as well as the formal consent form or script to be used to secure human subjects' agreement to participate in the study. And some readily grant exemption waivers to broad classes of non-intrusive research. It is wise to consult with a faculty member at your university with previous experience in human subjects research and in negotiating the IRB process, which often takes a few months to complete. So if you will collect data on or from people, be sure to start on this process as soon as you develop a reasonably clear idea of what your research design will look like.

The preparation for the actual fieldwork is often the part of the research that produces the greatest amount of anxiety. Uncertainty is at its highest just before one hits the ground. In the next chapter we address the actual landing.

4   Setting up to live and work

Having finally figured out where to go, you now have to plunge into the actual trip – a step fraught with apprehension. If this plunge has been preceded by a preparatory trip (see Chapter 2), established contacts and, hopefully, an understanding of the lay of the land at the research site will make the adjustment somewhat easier. Nevertheless, you do not usually know what to expect or have only a vague notion of possible problems. Even for those who have gone to the field on a preparatory research trip, getting started on the actual research is often a chore. The early stages of research are most taxing, particularly because you do not know what to expect or, in many cases, what exactly you are doing.

Once arriving in the field, it might take you weeks to figure out how to live and work. In this chapter on the initial stages of fieldwork, we take a practical look at some of the main issues involved in the transition.

Becoming familiar with an unfamiliar environment

Seasoned researchers commonly advise, "Don't expect to get much done during your first week or two." Even for undergraduate researchers (or others who may have a shorter time for the research and a less ambitious research project), there will be some set-up time associated with the research project. Above all, you will have to worry about practical things such as finding housing and arranging local finances. Taking care of such practical matters will demand most of your energy in the early stages. The difficulties associated with setting up in the field will depend both on how long you plan to stay and the particular research site. Despite the fact that such work is site-specific, one can generalize. Although Gretchen Bauer's account is specific to Namibia, she offers some broader lessons to those who have just arrived.

Box 4.1 Taking the time to acclimate

I arrived in Namibia at the beginning of December – a real down period in that country. It is the hottest time of the year and generally during the Christmas and New Year's holidays, the country just shuts down and people travel outside of the cities and towns – to the coast or to the north of the country. But it was just as well to arrive at this time because it takes a considerable amount of time to settle in and to familiarize oneself and one should allow oneself that time. Do not feel that you can or should begin your research the day after you arrive in-country. It is very important to take the time to set up a household and familiarize oneself before embarking on the much more difficult research enterprise. Thus I spent a fair amount of time setting up a household – obtaining furniture and buying pots and pans and blankets and so on. Also, one needs to learn one's way around – to buy a map and locate different relevant sites, to find out about public transport if there is any. It might be important to locate places where one can exercise – a swimming pool or track, for example. Similarly, one needs to know where to shop for various things – groceries, office supplies, etc. Also, one should check out the local media – radio, newspapers and television. These will undoubtedly be important sources of information – in one's research and in one's daily living. The idea is to integrate oneself as fully as possible. Skipping over settling-in things or rushing through them can have negative consequences later on. As a rule I think the things to do are very much the same things that one would do in any new environment. If you know anyone at your research site – no matter how little you might know them – contact them. It is also imperative to begin meeting people as soon as possible.

Gretchen Bauer

As Bauer notes, it often helps to check out the local media in the process of settling into the research site. Reading newspapers and watching television, reading online blogs by local commentators or listening to the radio in-country can help in several ways. In particular, it can improve your language ability, especially with local slang and colloquial expressions. It is also a very effective means of "getting inside" a local culture and political context. Paying attention to the popular media is one of the best ways to pick up the nuances and idiosyncrasies of any county or city or town.

Do not get frustrated at not being able to jump into the research immediately. Figuring out the right people to talk to is never easy, although a preparatory research trip certainly helps. Be patient at the beginning, realizing that much time will be taken up dealing with simply becoming situated. Above all, *listen*; since those you come into contact with (both for research purposes and practical purposes) will be likely to be interested in helping you, they will often have useful advice. You may not understand it the first time you hear it, so ask plenty of questions.

Money and housing

How do you take care of the practicalities of housing and money when in the field? Some of the relevant issues were addressed in the previous chapter on predeparture preparations. Nevertheless, you may want to make financial arrangements once in the field that make life easier. One of the options will be to set up a local bank account. Having a local bank account can make it much easier to pay bills and access money and is certainly safer than keeping money under the mattress, at least in many countries. The wisdom of setting up an account depends on the stability and reliability of the local financial system, as well as your location, the regulations placed on foreigners with bank accounts, and on the length of your stay in the field. Sometimes you will find that one bank branch tells you that setting up an account is "impossible" even when that is not true, while a helpful bank employee at another will ease the process. If you will be in the field for an extended period – and you determine that it's feasible and safe to set up an account – persistence may pay off.

You will also want to investigate the possibility of transferring funds from abroad. This can be more difficult than you might imagine, so contact banks in the United States before you leave for the field. One of the advantages of establishing a local bank account is that you will often be able to make the international transfer of funds simpler if it becomes necessary to do so. You should also keep in mind that some credit card companies will allow the cardholder to purchase traveler's checks with a check written on a home bank account. Finally, before you leave, locate the ATMs where you will be able to withdraw funds from your foreign bank account. Keep in mind, as well, that bank websites do not always give accurate information, so it is best to have a backup plan when it comes to accessing money.

As for housing, one of the recommendations in the previous chapter was to have some provisional plans set up when arriving in the field. In many cases, such a temporary arrangement will last only a few days. Assuming that you do not find your ideal home immediately, you will want to consider short-term arrangements in an apartment or house. In some cities, short-term leases (of a month, for example) are possible, and should be investigated. Moving to temporary quarters is likely to save a great deal of money, especially since an apartment or house is likely to have cooking facilities, which will spare the expense of eating out.

In finding more permanent arrangements, keep in mind that many countries have bureaucratic or legal hoops that might seem strange. For example, one researcher pointed out that in Guatemala, "foreigners need to have a local person, usually someone who owns property, to cosign rental agreements. This can sometimes be circumvented by paying several months' rent in advance, or providing other "guarantees" of your moral and financial standing. You should be prepared for this sort of bureaucratic obstacle, and understand that this is one of the reasons that the early period of research is the time when you will spend much of your money. The expense of setting up may at times seem excessive, but it is often the cost of doing research abroad.

Field-experienced researchers suggest a wide variety of ways to find housing. One strategy that is probably more reliable in urban areas is to check the classified ads in the local newspaper(s), or in local online sites (i.e. the local craigslist). If nothing else, this provides some idea of rental prices. Another way to find appropriate housing in urban areas is through a local real estate agent specializing in rental properties. Embassies sometimes have a list of such agents. Depending on the country, you may have to pay an agency fee, either a fixed sum or a percentage of the first month's rent. Regardless of whether the landlord or renter pays the fee, you will probably pay more through an agent. The agent is not going to do something for nothing. One researcher advised: "I would be cautious about renting through an agent after only a few days of looking. I think it is best to use the agents to help gain familiarity with the city, but then to check the fairness of their prices by asking local friends or checking newspaper ads." That said, one of the co-authors found an excellent house for a year-long rental through an agent, and although it may have cost slightly more than it would have done if the transaction did not have an intermediary, it reduced risk substantially. In addition, the rental agency intervened when repairs were needed, and had an incentive to keep both parties to the transaction happy.

Finally, one can rely on informal networks in finding housing, especially on the experience of researchers already in the field, and you may be able to occupy the dwelling of a fellow-researcher when they leave. These informal networks become broader and more reliable with more field time. As one contributor put it, "we relied on the *South American Handbook* for travel and lodging information at first, but the longer we stayed, the more we relied on personal contacts and accumulated knowledge." If you are patient (for example, by finding a temporary dwelling that you can put up with for a month), you will be much more likely to find satisfactory housing, especially in a city. Informal networks and contacts are even more important in rural areas, where the housing market may be thin or weak. They will also help you to understand which neighborhoods are more secure and which should be avoided.

Of course, what is satisfactory will depend on your circumstances and tastes. Most obviously, if you are alone, you may be willing to board with a family, as many single researchers do. Another scholar suggested that teacherages, dormitories for teachers, are an option, noting that "some secondary schools are anxious to keep their teacherages rented to bring in income." Generally speaking, singles can settle for somewhat more unusual circumstances, as Tyler Priest's vivid account demonstrates.

Box 4.2 The unexpected living arrangement

I arranged to rent a luxurious apartment in a high-rise Copacabana condo. The owners were an international buyer of bailer twine for a Minnesota agricultural cooperative and an offshore oilman working in Brazil for Zapata Oil (George Bush's former company). The buyer was a former Food for Peace worker in the 1960s; he gave up his humanitarianism but not his Brazilian contacts. The oilman was a former Peace Corps volunteer and AID field representative – a similar career trajectory. Both indulged heavily in the "exotic" aspects of Brazilian culture. The buyer even pictured himself as an American James Bond in Brazil (he admitted that his briefcase combination was 007). Thus, I found myself living in an apartment with beads hanging in doorways, mood lights, ceiling fans, and a waterbed built into the plushly carpeted bedroom floor. Despite my initial shock upon arriving at the apartment, I eventually grew quite fond of it. The owners, who visited occasionally, were interesting fellows who did have a lot of good advice about getting around in Rio. The rent for the apartment was a little higher than what I could have found elsewhere, but the place was secure, clean, and conveniently located.

Tyler Priest

With a family – and in particular with children – housing options are much more limited, and the search requires more patience. Many researchers found it useful to go to the field ahead of their families to secure permanent accommodations, since it can be tricky to search with a child or children in tow. Having some extra time to look for housing for the family can allow you to become familiar with local neighborhoods, schools, and day-care centers. Going ahead of the family is particularly advisable when you need to find temporary accommodations, most of which would not suit a family. That said, such a preliminary trip may not be financially feasible, and if it isn't, you will want to make sure to do as much research as possible to find adequate accommodations for when you first arrive on site.

Be wary of how locals perceive foreign researchers searching for housing. Although you are in a privileged position relative to most of the local population, most fieldworkers are not as rich as potential landlords may believe. As one scholar observed, "The highly competitive nature of the [housing] market and the belief on the part of many real estate agents that my pockets were stuffed with money made the search for an apartment a real nightmare." Such an experience is not at all unusual; be prepared for it. Research grants will not support the kinds of accommodations embassy personnel rent, but many locals will not differentiate between senior diplomats and undergraduate or graduate students.

An entirely separate and important issue concerns the interaction between your living arrangements and your research. Some research designs effectively dictate active involvement in the observed community. For example, it is hard to imagine fieldwork in social anthropology in which the researcher does not live smack in the middle of the subject population, often with a local family. Your choice of lodging can erect or reduce social barriers between the researcher and the locals. In most cultures, for instance, reciprocity is important, and an outsider living on her own, reasonably self-sufficiently, may be perceived as unintegrated into the complex local web of interdependence and thus as untrustworthy.

Bureaucratic and legal matters

In the previous chapter we discussed issues regarding research clearance and the necessity of delegating power of attorney at home. Here we address only the bureaucratic and legal matters you will be likely to confront in-country. Even if you received research clearance, there are often still bureaucratic hurdles to clear. In particular, you may have to register with the police or another internal security agency, often to receive a resident identity card or as a condition of research clearance. This is common not only in countries with authoritarian regimes; many countries are interested in keeping track of the doings of foreign researchers. As Karuna Morarji's account demonstrates, even citizens of the countries they are researching may have complications related to research clearance.

Box 4.3 Research clearance on site

I underestimated the difficulties of getting a research clearance from the Indian government. I had assumed that since I am an Indian citizen, and hence do not require a visa, I also would not need a clearance. I had heard that there were serious problems with getting Indian research clearances for a few years – with extensive delays and a lack of clarity about the process . . . But I thought that none of this would apply to me – until I realized that the agency which had given me a fellowship would only release the funding with a clearance, regardless of whether I needed it to go to India to start my research. The funding agency did not allow me to officially start my research without the clearance and would not pay for my travel to India, but I decided to take out a loan and go ahead, thinking that perhaps I could pursue the clearance process better on the ground, and that I could deal with some of the logistics of fieldwork while I was waiting. I left the US in August, expecting it might take a few months.

Nobody in New Delhi could tell me exactly what the problem was with the research clearance process for US-based scholars, but there clearly was a problem, and for some reason, somewhere in the bureaucracy, files were being 'held up.' I met a friend of a friend's who had recently helped someone's file 'move' – and get his clearance passed – but this person was not able to help me. I visited the US Educational Foundation India (the agency that had submitted the applications) offices and they reluctantly gave me my file number, and told me rather vaguely that they were doing everything possible to get clearances moving. But they were not hopeful, as there were still grant recipients from the previous year waiting for theirs . . .

The months passed, and I did not receive any news on my clearance. The funding agency extended their deadline for research start dates for all their India fellows. In April, more than six months after I had arrived in India, I received an email from a journalist at a major English-language newspaper in Delhi saying [that] he was contacting US-based scholars experiencing delays in research clearances for their 'stories,' and that he would appreciate hearing back from us. I sent him a detailed and passionate piece immediately, stressing that I was an Indian citizen and I still could not get a research clearance, that the procedure was ridiculously obscure and non-transparent, and that many scholars who care immensely for the country and have dedicated years of their lives to understanding its culture and society, learning its languages, etc., were being treated with more suspicion than multi-national corporations seeking to invest in India with purely profit-motivated intentions. The journalist phoned me the same evening, saying that he wanted to publish parts of my piece in the following day's paper. The next day, my photo and 'story' was on the front page of the paper! It turned out that it was the first piece in a week-long special feature on the issue of research clearance delays. Within a few days, I heard from USEFI that my clearance should be coming through within days, and I did indeed receive it just a couple of days later.

Without the prominent media attention, who knows when or even if I would have received the clearance. Indian friends had advised me to go to the press earlier as often it is the most efficient form of public pressure, but I had worried about antagonizing the concerned government department. Figuring out how to take any action in a situation like this is tricky.

Karuna Morarji

As Karuna makes clear, her ultimate strategy of going to the media worked, but such a strategy would only work in some places, some times, and carries significant risk. In the end, the particular resolution to this saga is less crucial in terms of the lessons learned than is the understanding that research clearance, in some places, may present serious obstacles even when a researcher is in-country.

One other bureaucratic matter to take care of is registration with one's home country embassy or consulate, as embassies are interested in knowing the whereabouts of visiting nationals and can provide valuable services in case of emergency. So it is wise to register with your embassy as well. It is generally easy to do so on the web; for researchers from the US, one can register at: https://travelregistration.state.gov/ibrs/ui/

Some countries are also particularly concerned with what foreign researchers bring in for research purposes. In many cases, after some paper-work, a research visa makes it relatively easy to bring in needed equipment. Keep in mind that the chief concern of trade bureaucracies is that you might sell the imported equipment illegally, thereby undermining local customs laws. We return to these issues in Chapter 5.

In addition, you may need to deal with the local immigration departments to renew a visa or to change your visa status. Needless to say, this can be a frustrating experience, or, for one contributor, almost a surreal one:

> I can say without exaggeration that I went through over two dozen different trips to different government offices and ministries, and all of that without any objection or opposition to my request for renewal of my visa. It was simply a Kafkaesque experience of being sent from one functionary to another, each of whom added to the list of requirements or claimed that I had come to the wrong place. At one point, when an official told me that I had come to the wrong office, even though an official in a different ministry insisted that that was where I was supposed to go, and told me instead to go to a Ministry across town, I asked if he was certain. He replied that I had offended him by doubting him. So I dutifully went off to the ministry to which he directed me, only to be told that I had gone to the wrong place and was sent somewhere else.

Faced with such situations, you may be tempted to offer a bribe to an obstructing official. After all, many researchers carry to the field a stereotype of the relatively corrupt foreign official, and might figure that a few well-placed bills will grease the bureaucratic wheels and allow them to get on with their work. This stereotype is often inaccurate and the strategy is perilous, in both ethical and practical terms. We strongly recommend against attempts at bribery. Even if such practices seem common in the host country, foreigners rarely know what they are doing; bribery is, after all, a rather complicated cultural practice. Bribery carries with it real risks. A foreigner with substantial resources who breaks the law is an easy target. You may consider yourself savvy in offering a bribe, but usually you are simply being stupid, and once you head down the road of bribery, many other complications commonly ensue.

With family in the field

As noted in the previous chapter, going to the field with the family poses special challenges. A number of the important issues regarding family in the field were tackled in Chapter 3, so here we briefly address one issue in particular: finding day care or schools for children in the field.

If accompanied to the field by children, you almost certainly have to arrange for day care, schooling, or both. Although it is difficult to arrange these from abroad, you may be able to make some valuable contacts – with potential schools or day-care centers – via email. One researcher with a small child pointed out that although you might be reluctant to place a small child in day care when abroad, it can provide the child with some continuity if he or she is already used to a day-care environment. It may also be necessary when both parents are working on research and/or writing. Finally, having kids in school or day care may open up social options for the parents, who also happen to be researchers, and can provide great opportunities for the children to make good linguistic progress at a point when their minds are particularly open to learning a new language.

A number of researchers pointed out that some sort of home day care is often feasible, although it might be difficult to get used to the idea of having domestic help. Indeed, while many researchers instinctively feel uncomfortable employing domestic help, there are several reasons to do so. The first is time. "If you always cook for yourself," observed one contributor, "you might be taking valuable time away from your work. I tried to cook for myself at first, but the challenges of transforming food from its unprocessed form to something nutritious and edible in one pot proved to be too much for me. I eventually hired a young girl to come and cook in the evenings for me, which enabled me to get in a good three hours more of research time." The second reason to employ domestic help is employment creation. Whether or not you deplore the economic structure that leads to a large class of unemployed and underemployed in your research site, refusing to employ domestic help on "moral" grounds neither changes that structure nor provides jobs to those who need them.

Setting up schooling for children can be a daunting task, and quite naturally makes parents uneasy. One seasoned researcher noted that he and his wife took quite a bit of time at the beginning of his research period to find an appropriate school for their first-grader. They ended up visiting more than half a dozen schools before settling on one. A number of factors entered into their decision-making process, including cost, the language spoken in the school, and the quality of the education. As for cost, bear in mind that schools for foreigners are often prohibitively expensive for the researcher on a limited budget. Many of these schools cater to the children of foreign diplomats and international businesspersons, most of whose employers pay for their children's education. You should think seriously about the language in which classes will be taught. Some will prefer schools that teach in English, so as to ease the transition for the child. At the same time, the cost of English-speaking schools is usually greater. The quality of educational systems in most developing countries varies greatly (often more so than it does at home). More often than not, foreign researchers enroll their children in private schools abroad.

Finally, be aware that the adjustment to a new school in a new country with a new language can be extremely difficult for a child. Be alert to the stress that it might cause for your child. As one researcher pointed out, at the beginning of the research period the child may be unable to handle many things previously taken for granted, for example, the ability to cope with the cruelties that children inevitably inflict on one another. Like adults, children often feel defenseless if they cannot verbalize. So, consider some elementary language lessons for your child before going to the field.

Lest we emphasize the negative too much, we should note that children are often the greatest beneficiaries of research abroad. They learn about a new culture, often learn a new language, and learn, of necessity, how important it is to be flexible. One of the co-authors brought three children abroad (ages 16, 11, and 3 at the time) for a year, and they all, in their own way, found this to be a life-changing experience, even though (they would all say) it was quite stressful and daunting at times. But in the end, it was an incredibly positive experience.

Issues of gender, race, class, and age

Gender, race class, and age have a profound effect on both setting up in the field and in the actual fieldwork itself. Simply put, people react differently to men and women, to persons of different skin color, and to older and younger researchers, and the quality of your research will be affected by the differences in response.

To begin with gender, being a woman can cut both ways when doing fieldwork. In the words of one female researcher, "I found that my gender role actually helped my research experience – as a woman, people saw me as less threatening than a male researcher." Such perceptions of women are probably common in many countries and, however misplaced, can be used to advantage. In a similar vein, both men and women in the research site may feel that the single woman alone needs "protection and assistance," which can often prove valuable in practical terms during the rigors of fieldwork, as a number of women contributors pointed out.

There are, of course, distinct disadvantages to being a woman in the field. Some of these disadvantages are personal; others are academic. Women often have to deal with harassment, and as one scholar who did her work in Latin America pointed out, "women who are not from Los Angeles or New York have to get used to the way men are expected to hiss at women in the street." This same researcher also noted wryly that single women in particular can have problems finding housing: "People are reluctant to rent to single females, especially North Americans, because [they say] we have no morals." Needless to say, the power of stereotypes, especially with the transmission of images in our globalized media, is often difficult to overcome, especially in cultures where one is an outsider.

Professionally and academically, gender can affect one's access to informants. As one researcher reported, "When I told [male] agronomists that I was doing my work on women in agriculture, they invariably steered me towards the widows, as if these were the only category of women working in agriculture." Similarly, a male researcher may be encouraged to talk only to men, which can obviously bias research conclusions, or, if he is trying to study work that women do, he may face different obstacles. One male scholar noted that because he was doing research on household economic practices and would need to interview mainly women, he found it necessary and useful to hire a female research assistant and female enumerators once in the field. These circumstances are hardly unusual. It is essential to remain aware that gender frequently influences the kind and source of information that is provided. As another scholar noted, "It would be hard to conceive of a research topic in which gender did not matter somehow.... Male and female perceptions and experiences of similar things are frequently very different, and one can rarely have a complete and full picture without interviewing people of both sexes."

Some women noted how gender interacts with race to produce unexpected outcomes about which other women should be aware. Laura Hammond discusses her experience in the field.

Box 4.4 Gender, race, and the outside researcher

It is difficult to say whether my gender helped me in my efforts to settle in. I suppose it did, for I was a single woman, on my own, and therefore by the conventions of Tigrayan [Ethiopian] society I was in need of protection and assistance. On the other hand, I am not convinced that some of the villagers ever really considered me to be fully female. To many I think I was sort of a nongendered creature. One woman even grabbed my breasts to see if I really had any! Many people could not understand how I could have reached the age of 27 without having gotten married or had children. As a white woman I could balance both gender roles. I could interview men in the houses where local beer was brewed and sold, places forbidden to respectable women, but I could also sit with women in their homes and discuss intimate aspects of childbirth, a subject which was off-limits to men. As I got to know people better, they came to accept me as having definite differences from Tigrayan women, but as female nonetheless.

Laura Hammond

The disadvantages of gender are sometimes neutralized by the advantages of race and class. As one woman put it, "Being a foreign woman tends to protect one in those instances where [native] women might be discriminated against or disadvantaged." The particular research site and topic will determine the degree to which disadvantages can be offset or turned into advantages. As another researcher pointed out, "It is of course difficult to tease out the effects of gender from those of race, nationality, and class in assessing my experiences in the field. Equally it is impossible to know if and how I might have been treated differently if I were a man."

Most researchers also confront class differences. While most student researchers feel far from rich when conducting their fieldwork, they are usually better off than the vast majority of the developing country population where they are studying, which, as one researcher pointed out, warrants special sensitivity:

> In some cultures, this status implies certain expectations of reciprocity and generosity that one should familiarize oneself with. People may sometimes have certain expectations of you that may be unrealistic, but necessitate some gestures that indicate that you are not oblivious to them. . . . Even though students may not feel that they are "rolling in the dough," they often are not fully aware of how wealthy they are in comparison to many of their counterparts in their host country.

Indeed, academics in many developing countries must live with uncertainty about job stability, and in many countries these academics have to hold down several jobs to make ends meet. Sensitivity to this reality makes the research process smoother and more productive.

Finally, the age of the researcher and local assumptions about what is expected of people of a particular age affect access to informants and social treatment. Like class and race, age can neutralize the disadvantages of gender in many cultures. One female researcher, discussing sexual harassment, made observations and suggested strategies "to minimize these unpleasant interactions": "The older you are, the less prone you are to such abuses. It is also how you dress. The more 'professional,' businesslike and mature [-looking] your clothes, the less likely you are to evoke such reactions." Ortbals and Rincker (2009: 315) also note the way in which age and gender intersect: "the embodied experience of a young woman researcher does not effortlessly coincide with what she hopes to feel like as an accomplished researcher." Researchers who do not "fit" a preconceived cultural notion of what researchers are supposed to look like will have to come to develop strategies to overcome (or ameliorate) this disjunction between what researchers think they are and what the informants think they are.

More generally, female researchers must get used to the fact that they will often be viewed as suspect because of their chosen career path. Indeed, Hammond's descriptions (above) demonstrate not only the effects of race and gender, but age as well. She points out that she was considered an oddity because she had not gotten married or had children by the ripe old age of 27. As another scholar observed in this regard, "In the United States, grad students often have to postpone marriage and children for the sake of their studies or they may choose not to marry or have children for various reasons. Yet these life choices may be regarded with suspicion among people one is working with abroad. . . . I have observed how a lack of sensitivity to these age grades and life experiences can at times lead to serious breakdowns in communication." Strategies for coping with these inevitable differences include observing the behavior of others very carefully, and asking locals with whom you feel comfortable (friends of a similar age, or your language instructor, for example) about proper etiquette. One contributor also suggested setting aside time when first conducting an interview to let respondents ask questions about you, as this can lead to interesting discussions and can help break the ice and lead respondents to be more open with the researcher.

Relations with expatriates

At some point in the research (often at the beginning), you will be confronted with the presence, social opportunities, and demands of expatriates in the field. There are no hard and fast rules or advice to give when one deals with fellow foreigners. The experiences of researchers overseas with expatriate communities varies widely.

On the positive side, expatriates can be useful for making contacts in the field – both social and academic – and these contacts are usually most useful in the early stages of research. Other scholars in your field can help with seasoned information regarding contacts, housing, financial matters, potential informants, local research institutions, and local libraries and archives. Foreign researchers can also help you test ideas in the formative stage, since fellow researchers are usually familiar with academic cultures at home. Many expatriates returning home, on leave or permanently, quite willingly serve as couriers when you need to send things back to the US before your research time has concluded.

Contacts with expatriates can also help in the logistics of fieldwork. One scholar's contacts with other foreign researchers helped to determine how and how much to pay research team members, a reasonable work schedule, and where to recruit potential research team members. Contact with other foreigners doing research in the field also provides information on what others are doing, which can provide for intellectual stimulation and is a way to avoid the potential disaster of duplicating another's research.

Finally, on a social level, befriending other expatriates can offer some balance to life during an intense period. One colleague noted that while most of his friends in the field were local, he and his wife found it possible to "let their hair down" with a good friend who hailed from the United States. Contact with those from your own culture can provide a needed and helpful break from the grind of fieldwork and a soothing cultural touchstone.

There are, nonetheless, drawbacks to spending a lot of time with foreigners in the field. While socializing with expatriates can help, one contributor remarked that "to alleviate the inevitable sense of isolation, . . . ex-pat communities tend to be clannish, incestuous, hived-off from local society – to exhibit all the characteristics of very small towns." You will have many fewer opportunities to immerse yourself in local culture and language if you hang out with expatriates too much. Given that much good research is done through such immersion, and the opportunities it provides, spending time with expats can delay real understanding of your local environment.

When it comes to dealing with other segments of the expatriate society – officials at the embassy or foreign aid missions, for example – most researchers recommend some distance. One wrote, "I tried to stay away from the Embassy folks as much as possible. They are a very insular group; those who live in the embassy compound usually do not go out very often, and they generally haven't spent much time in the rest of the country." Below, Gretchen Bauer sums up a feeling expressed by a number of researchers. There are good reasons to be careful of relationships with expatriate communities, especially when they are "official."

Box 4.5 Relationships with expatriate communities

I think it can be a real trap to associate too strongly with any of the expatriate communities. They tend to live in considerable isolation from the people of the country they live in – and yet believe they know what is going on because they talk to their domestic workers, gardeners, drivers and other employees. While the old suspicions toward Americans, and especially anyone associated with the official community seem to have waned somewhat, efforts to live among the people of a country rather than with fellow expatriates are enormously appreciated and certainly infinitely more rewarding for the researcher. At the same time, one must tread carefully. Especially if one has US government funds (e.g. as a Fulbright Scholar) one must learn what is expected by the embassy or US Information Service office and must certainly avoid antagonizing anyone. I think cordial but cool relations can be the best unless, of course, one wants more. A drawback of associating with the Embassy or USIS people is that they, recognizing their own dearth of information, may attempt to get more information from those researchers they know to be well-acquainted with the local scene. Here it is especially important not to betray any confidences of one's respondents. The official community hires its own people to obtain information and they should not be after researchers – even those from their country – for such input.

Gretchen Bauer

Bear in mind Bauer's point that researchers with US government funds may need the official community for things such as visa renewal, use of the diplomatic pouch, or access to the embassy health clinic. Thus, be careful not to alienate those who can provide such services. It should also be noted that researchers report a rather wide variety of experiences with expatriate officials. Some can be extraordinarily helpful, others can be mostly a hindrance. Whatever the specific circumstances, exercise some caution in your dealings with officials.

A comment on expatriates by a scholar who has worked in North Africa captures some of the ways in which such communities can provide another perspective:

> I have found US expatriates to be some of the most bizarre, eccentric, and, therefore, entertaining people I have ever met. They're always weird or unique in some way. We enjoyed socializing with Americans, sharing ideas, arguing, drinking. Government folks – USIS, USAID, American Embassy – were especially interesting to spend time with. They were sources of information, and it was fascinating to listen to their views of Tunisia and Tunisians. Many of them, shall we say, live in an enclave. They had guards and drivers, they shopped at the commissary, they avoided learning Arabic. Yet they had ample opinions about Tunisians. It was interesting to observe their behavior.

However you choose to approach the expatriate community – as an obstacle, a source of support, or an object of study – expatriates are just one small part of a fascinating puzzle.

Finally, you should keep in mind that there is a flipside to trying to avoid expats, should you choose to do so. Kasia Paprocki illustrates the nuances and complexities associated with trying to avoid them in her field narrative.

Box 4.6 Straddling cultures

When we arrived in Bangladesh, my partner and I agreed that we were committed to developing relationships only with locals, living in neighborhoods where expats didn't live, and generally living a lifestyle that was as close to that of most Bangladeshis as possible. Our limited experiences with tank-top-wearing expats in the diplomatic enclave turned us off from the small but strong expat community and we made a conscious effort not to spend time with these people. We became very close with a local family and moved in next door to them. We learned more from the experience of getting to know this family than any other aspect of our research and time abroad. However, after some time living this way we discovered tensions between living like and with a local family and concentrating on our research. Staying up late playing with children often got in the way of writing daily field notes, and we had a hard time asking to be left alone to concentrate on our work and writing. Opening ourselves and our home up to these new friends meant that they often showered and did laundry at our house, made meals in our kitchen, and stored food in our refrigerator. We were expected to fast with them during Ramadan and to pay visits with them to the homes of their friends and relatives. Ultimately, we realized that we could not "live like them" and still accomplish everything we were there to do. When we later met a small group of like-minded researchers, we were thrilled to realize the joys of having other people to relate to, and realized that we were really missing something without this. It was great to have people to be "tourists" with occasionally, to visit historical and cultural sites that our Bangladeshi friends might not be interested in. We found that having the opportunity to process our experiences with other foreigners meant a great deal to us, and helped us to make the most of our time abroad. While it's clear that we would have missed out on a lot if we had associated only with the small and insular expatriate community, finding a good balance can mean a lot to one's overall happiness and comfort overseas.

Kasia Paprocki

Maintaining sanity in the field

The fieldwork experience is almost always intense, and can be trying as you attempt to get used to a new environment while concurrently working at what is often breakneck speed. Resources and time are limited, and so you may be tempted to work all of the time so as to not let opportunities slip by. Nevertheless, almost all experienced field researchers highly recommend taking regular breaks. A vacation can be rejuvenating and often makes you more productive in the long term. As one researcher put it, "Before I started my fieldwork, I had a vision of staying in my field site for months and months at a time," but this vision soon gave way to the need for real breaks. This researcher went on to note that "I used to feel guilty about taking these breaks. I felt that I wasn't a real anthropologist unless I was in the thick of it all the time. Finally I made peace with the fact that I needed the breaks and that I work better if I can get out for a while. I come back refreshed, often with new ideas, and with new enthusiasm for the research." Another researcher recommended taking a vacation around the middle of the research trip, since it often becomes increasingly difficult to break away near the end of the stay. Some occasional cooling off is needed when running at full tilt, as inevitably occurs deep into your field time.

It is especially important for people who are on their own to take the occasional break from work. You might be even more tempted to work all of the time when alone and anxious to return home to loved ones, but it is not advisable. The absence of a companion with whom to share ideas often discourages critical reflection on the research experience in progress. Moreover, the fatigue of incessant work only worsens the emotional challenges faced by a homesick fieldworker. A break can be of even greater value under such circumstances.

Many researchers pointed out the importance of exercise in the field. Aside from helping with physical endurance (Ortbals and Rincker, 2009: 315–16), keeping a regular exercise routine in the field can help to clear one's mind for work. That said, several problems crop up as you attempt to keep up a regular exercise routine in the field. The most important limitation is the dearth of facilities in many places. Northern researchers grow accustomed to universities with excellent athletic facilities for which they do not have to pay, at least explicitly. Such arrangements are highly unusual in most developing countries. More often than not, the only good facilities are private clubs, which can be expensive and often beyond the researcher's financial means. You may have to come up with alternatives to gym facilities for exercise. If you run regularly, pay attention to personal safety. Even if you have to be concerned about personal safety at home, you are also much more familiar with your home environment. Driving habits, the conditions of roads, sidewalks and the air, leashing and vaccination of dogs, and other environmental differences can affect the running experience (sometimes dramatically). Biking and swimming are sometimes popular and financially feasible options, although health and safety cautions still pertain.

Finally, several scholars noted the importance of writing – email letters sent to friends and/or family, or a journal, or a blog or Facebook or other social networking site – as a way to release tension and gain insight into the research process. As one put it, "I enjoy writing and also receiving letters ... I shared experiences and newspaper clippings and a few things from Thailand with my family and friends at home. They responded in kind, and as I have looked back over the correspondence I can see that it is really very hard to separate personal from professional issues in international research." Writing socially, not just academically, provides an opportunity to reflect on the research experience and can help in the process of discernment of researcher strategies and accomplishments.

Settling in academically

Up to this point, we have been concerned with very practical issues of settling in to do research. Nonetheless, after the initial settling-in period, you must figure out how to get on with work. This can be quite difficult, charting unknown territory on your own, often doing original research for the first time. In this last section, we discuss some of the ways in which you can get moving productively.

First, a few words on protocol and personal comportment. One of the most offensive things that you can do is to arrive on site and begin making demands on local academic institutions, for example, demanding immediate access to the internet, office space, or administrative services. One researcher noted that "the researcher [should] exercise some cultural sensitivity. Quiet observation may avert errors that can be costly to a researcher. In many countries in West Africa, personal relations are critical for the success or failure of a project. Warm greetings, remembering to ask about families, and immersing oneself in the culture may allow for a truly productive research experience." The importance of personal relations extends far beyond West Africa. As this researcher pointed out, common courtesy and sensitivity to the local way of doing things can be both personally and professionally rewarding. Keep in mind that "cold professionalism" is not necessarily appropriate, as it often is at home. This does not mean that you should spend all of your time on small talk, but it does mean that jumping straight into academic discussions can turn people off. The best way to figure out what is and is not appropriate is to listen and observe when you first arrive in the field. And, as Christian Lentz notes, it can be helpful to participate in activities to which your hosts invite you.

Box 4.7 Dancing in the archives

All archival access is restricted, whether because of secrecy or time constraints. Working within these limits demands patience and flexibility. On my first day in Vietnam's national archives, the reading room manager said that the collections were opening up, and that my only limit was time.

At first, I worried whether time I spent in the archives not reading was useful. Every day I drank tea in the manager's office, ate fruit with his staff, and chatted about life in the US and Hanoi.

One day over tea, the woman who delivered my folders asked if I was coming to dance class that afternoon. Dance class – in the archives?! I agreed reluctantly. Later, when I turned in my folders, the beat was already pulsing. Downstairs, those people who, hours earlier, had acted so officiously were now paired up, smiling broadly, and cutting the rug. An instructor counted out numbers and demonstrated steps. Someone led me in the Rumba. My attempts elicited cheers. That I danced with two left feet, however, perplexed my partner: 'You're from the southern US, right, close to Cuba? Then why can't you dance?'

Over these lessons and teas, I grew to know the staff, on whose labors my research depended, as people. Back in the reading room, they no longer looked at my requests somberly, but accepted them with the smiles we shared on the dance floor. Even if my own feet remained stiff, my flexibility earned me new friends, improving my access and work.

Christian Lentz

It is, indeed, advisable to loosen up one's expectation of "work" at the outset, and take time to explore different ways of integrating with host institutions and their own work culture. At the same time, it is important to note that boundaries are often different when doing research abroad. Reinhardt (2009: 296) notes that when doing research in Brazil, "The interviews I did conduct often resulted in invitations to parties and social functions . . . Gamely, I attended as many of these functions as possible . . . People with no interest in returning my phone calls, upon meeting me at a party, would instantly invite me to their office the next day. Since I was invited to these functions by men and women alike, and regularly sensed that my decision to attend might help me pass a test of my sincerity and commitment to the person who had invited me, I was naïve to the idea that a young woman at a party might connote any image other than that of a researcher." Reinhardt later notes that this willingness to mix work and the social led to some unwanted advances, and it is worth noting that any researcher – male or female, gay or straight – should be aware of the potential complications of mixing work and social activities while in the field.

Above all, most seasoned researchers counsel patience in the early stages of research. You will not get everything done immediately. You are likely to go down more than a few dead-end paths. Becoming familiar with the ins and outs of a particular research context takes time; there is often no way to rush the process. Many scholars fear that not much is being accomplished during the beginning stages of the research. This is normal. Do not become unnecessarily alarmed.

If you arranged affiliation with a research institution before going to the field, one of the first things to do after arriving in-country is to visit the institution. As we noted in the previous chapter, the benefits of affiliation can vary greatly, from an office and administrative support to an affiliation in name only. If at all possible, attempt to become involved in the institutional life early in the process of doing research. One scholar became immediately and actively involved in her research institute. Indeed, she ended up organizing a weekly seminar series on research in progress by the host institute's researchers and had a very positive experience with the affiliate.

Others are not so lucky, and find involvement in institutional life practically impossible. Some places do not have much of an institutional life. As one researcher pointed out: "My research affiliation and relations with the (few) Honduran scholars did not progress as anticipated. I found not [a single] student or professor who was really interested in my topic or anxious for research collaboration or shared authorship of an article."

If you have not set up an affiliation with a local research institution before going to the field, you should still visit local institutions to make contacts. This is an appropriate courtesy to extend to professional colleagues. Moreover, such contacts often prove beneficial, especially when made early enough in the research period to make good use of them.

If you intend to use local libraries and archives, visit as many of these places as possible in the early stages of research. Establish what is and what is not available, during what hours, and on which days. Try to determine which places are likely to have more useful information and deserve further exploration. Talk to the librarians or archivists at these institutions to find out what might be available that is not necessarily obvious. Unless you stumble onto a gold mine in the early stages of research, it is probably not advisable to spend too much time in any one place initially. Those who adopt a narrowing strategy too soon often later come to regret their blinders. Getting a broad lay of the land can help one feel productive and able to figure out what is available, and can help the process of narrowing or refining the research project early on.

Finally, a good and generalizable piece of advice offered by a researcher who spent two years in the field is to get to know as many people as possible: "I decided very early on that it was important that I first meet as many people as possible socially and that these social acquaintances could later be transformed into working relationships. I also realized early on that it would be quite some time before I felt in a position to conduct personal interviews, which meant that I had the time to spend in cultivating these relationships first." Not everyone will have the luxury of a long period of fieldwork, but it is important to keep in mind that any trip may be the first time of many. Concern yourself with cultivating personal relationships for the long run.

5   The logistics of fieldwork

Some experienced field researchers suggest, with a mixture of amusement and exasperation, that fieldwork is one part intellectual exploration and ten parts daily maintenance. Even in the security of your home university, you inevitably spend far more time handling administrative details, financial matters, minor and major crises concerning computers, cell phones or other equipment, and personal and familial arrangements than is anticipated or desired. When displaced to a foreign culture, the non-academic demands on time multiply. More rudimentary communications and transportation infrastructure, unfamiliar legal and administrative procedures, and the challenges of working in a foreign language often seem to rob overseas field researchers of the time they need to get on with the study. But do not despair; these experiences are part of what makes overseas research so rich. Logistical hiccups are a universal experience for which the best advice is to be flexible and patient. However, knowing how others have handled common problems and with what results may be helpful to your and your project's daily maintenance.

In this chapter we confront the myriad logistical issues involved in establishing and executing a field research project overseas. Few will need to consider all the subsidiary issues addressed here. Indeed, a fortunate minority will not concern themselves with vehicles or other equipment more uncommon than a cell phone or laptop, nor will they need research assistants. But the vast majority of researchers confront such issues, and many devise fairly ingenious solutions to the challenges they encounter. Although these challenges sometimes prove exasperating, they are also an important, even potentially enjoyable part of the research process. As one scholar put it, "A sense of humor is very important. When I complained to a Moroccan friend that I had trouble with local, dialectical Arabic and Berber, she responded that people will always help you – despite language and cultural barriers – if they sense kindness, humor, and honesty."

Research equipment

Although student field research rarely demands elaborate laboratories filled with expensive and delicate equipment, even the simplest research designs today depend on some basic tools: computers, digital recorders, cameras, photocopiers, cell phones and the like. You need to think through the necessary equipment at an early stage, determine whether it is better to bring needed items along or to acquire them on site, and plan for maintenance.

Most field researchers consider a computer essential. It undoubtedly makes the research process more organized and efficient. As one researcher notes emphatically, you "should be writing in a journal or keeping regular notes constantly, every free minute you have. If it is inputted into the computer, this saves many hours [later], since you can, through various search methods, find key words and files in seconds once you start writing up." You can code, enter, clean, and even analyze data in the field, permitting follow-up correctives when necessary. Having a computer also helps begin the process of writing, and many experienced researchers think starting to write while still in the field is a very good idea.

Equipment size and portability matter. The more portable the laptop, the better. If the power fails, most laptops automatically switch to battery power, virtually all laptops today handle either 110 or 220 volt electrical systems, and many have rudimentary surge protection built in as well. Be sure to invest in as much (random access) memory (RAM) as you can afford and in a good wireless adapter. As one respondent put it, "I don't know how people used to do field research without laptops." But also beware of the distortionary effects a laptop can have on one's research in settings where computers are rare. As one student who worked in poor communities in rural India remarked, "The couple of times that I [took my laptop to the village with me], the trip ended up centered around my laptop and not the research." Another remarked that "in my experience, electronic equipment only adds to the barrier a researcher is trying to break down."

Opinions vary on what peripherals to bring along. Many experienced field researchers recommend a portable external hard drive on which one can back up essential data for off-site storage. We discuss data security issues further in Chapter 6.

The other commonly recommended computer peripheral is a lightweight, portable printer that also functions as a scanner (all-in-one printer/scanner/copiers are commonplace and inexpensive). It can be very difficult to locate, much less gain access to, functioning computer printers in many low-income countries. One noted, "Although computers are widespread in the Philippines, decent printers are not always easy to find. Having one allows me some autonomy and [allows me] to reserve asking favors for other needs." But at least one researcher took a printer that caused her considerable mechanical difficulty and proved to be just added weight and hassle. Others found their printing needs minimal and access to borrowed printers sufficient. Nonetheless, we concur with most scholars who recommend taking a printer to the field. Remember, however, that replacement printer cartridges are often difficult to find, especially for more obscure model printers, so take a spare with you and order a replacement right away if and when the first one runs out.

One political scientist doing archival work in Chile stumbled across several thousand pages of valuable documents that he was not permitted to photocopy and for which he wanted the text, not just notes. Fortunately, he was able to borrow a hand-held scanner from another foreign researcher. "The results were amazing. In a week and a half I had all the documents entered into my computer and printed out in hard copy." Indeed, the archivists were so impressed with the results that they set about obtaining a scanner for the library. For those doing much archival work, a portable scanner (as distinct from a scanner on your printer) may be a worthwhile investment, saving transcription time, photocopying expenses, and the weight of hard copies in one's luggage.

There is no simple rule as to whether or not to take computer peripherals. Consider your likely needs for printing, scanning, communications, data backup; the availability of such peripherals on site; and the costs of carrying, maintaining, and protecting the equipment. Then make a decision appropriate to the circumstances of the research project. If you do take peripherals, assemble and test the whole system at your home institution prior to departure to facilitate identification and resolution of hardware or software conflicts that can bedevil fieldwork. One researcher lamented that because he did not buy and test his computer and printer together before leaving the United States, a small software problem that could have been corrected in a matter of minutes at home took several months to solve in Uganda.

The laptop's only rival as the most essential field research equipment is the cell phone. They are ubiquitous nearly everywhere, and it is best to buy one locally – or just buy a local SIM card to fit into your own phone if it is compatible with the local system – as opposed to relying on the (usually very expensive) international roaming capabilities of the cell phone you use at home.

Other equipment that contributing researchers mentioned as particularly useful included cameras, video cameras and monitors (for making a visual record of sites and events), digital recorders and transcription machines (for making verbatim records of interviews), and scales (for anthropometric data collection). The needs of any particular project clearly vary with the work style of the researcher, the question at hand, and the environment in which the study is conducted. Talk to others who have worked in the same setting or who have undertaken similar studies about what equipment is essential, what would be handy, and what is unnecessary.

The decision of whether to bring equipment along or to buy it on site generally turns on four issues: the relative price of the item(s) at home and in the host country, and your access to funds with which to make equipment purchases before departure; differences in the quality of equipment available in the different locations; government or grantsmaker restrictions on cross-border movement of equipment; and international differences in equipment design and functionality. In all but a very few cases, equipment is cheaper, of better quality, and of greater variety in North America or Europe than in low- or middle-income countries, and is legally transportable across borders. Most researchers therefore take their equipment with them.

With some notable exceptions, most low-income countries import consumer electronics (for example, computers, cameras, digital recorders), so such items often cost more in the host country than at home. The price differentials are sometimes dramatic, especially where foreign exchange flows are restricted or the government imposes heavy import tariffs on luxury items. No matter how necessary it might seem to the itinerant researcher, most of the world's population still considers a laptop computer a luxury.

Check to see what restrictions the host country customs service places on items brought in. Some countries suspect that imported electronics, such as computers, will be sold in-country and, thus, tax them as imports. These duties can be enormous. If there is no duty, there may well be restrictions on subsequent sale. Talk with researchers recently in-country or with embassy officials before your departure. It is often handy to have proof of purchase and a letter from some official body (e.g, a funding agency, host or home institution) indicating that the equipment is for research purposes only and will not be sold.

Since purchasing power is limited in poorer countries, selection is often very limited for items such as laptop computers and digital recorders. Also, the quality of available models may not meet your expectations or needs. Given price and quality differences, in most cases it seems far more cost-effective to take along necessary advanced research equipment rather than to purchase items on site.

This discussion also raises the broader question of product price/quality tradeoffs. Inexperienced field researchers too often err on the side of sacrificing necessary quality in an effort to conserve scarce funds. This often comes back to haunt them, as Dan Maxwell points out.

Box 5.1 Price/quality tradeoffs in critical equipment

Even on simple things, it is not worth trying to save a few dollars. I didn't want to take my good stapler, for example, because I thought I might lose it. So I bought the best I could get locally, and was never able to staple together more than six or seven sheets of paper – again, not a large frustration, but I had to assemble 720 fifteen-page questionnaires over the course of three months with a lousy stapler that didn't work. The examples go on and on, but the message should be simple: Don't cut corners on basic necessary equipment.

Dan Maxwell

Some grantsmakers (for example, US government agencies) insist or strongly suggest equipment purchases should be made at home prior to departure. Your decision of where to purchase necessary equipment might thus be made by a third party. There can also be the matter of cross-cultural differences in equipment design. For example, if you need a computer that will be used by an assistant unfamiliar with European script, the appropriate equipment may be easier and cheaper to acquire on site than in Europe or North America. In a similar spirit, one contributor doing anthropometric surveying "purchased a very accurate scale for body weight in the US and shipped it to Swaziland. It would have been far easier on me and the poor scale to have gotten it in South Africa. It was eventually donated to the Ministry of Agriculture and Coops [per donor guidelines on disposal of durable equipment] but since it was in pounds, not grams, its usefulness for them is somewhat dubious. A good example of a bad guess!"

Keep in mind that all equipment requires maintenance, some of which will inevitably exceed your abilities. Mechanical difficulties can drain your time, patience, and funds if your location lacks parts or technicians. For that reason, brand choice can be important. Unless you are working in urban areas of reasonably technologically advanced countries, it is wise to establish which manufacturers have service representatives, warranty repair facilities, and parts suppliers reasonably proximate to your research site. Several scholars bought a particular make of computer expressly because of service availability in the research site. Remember that many warranties are voided if an unauthorized technician services the equipment.

That said, the quality of the service ultimately depends on the local staff, who might not be well trained, well compensated, or highly motivated. The physical presence of a licensed warranty service center does not mean they can or will actually fix your equipment there. It is wise to clarify the terms of the warranty in advance and bring along the necessary documentation. But be forewarned that even reputable companies do not always honor warranties overseas. You can, however, almost always contact technical support or customer service at home if local technicians cannot solve the problem.

Be prepared with spare parts or even spare equipment. One researcher's pocket recorder was stolen in Namibia and she had to buy a second one at a substantially higher price. Parts and supplies for equipment, if available at all, are often quite a bit more expensive overseas and of substantially lower quality. Even simple things, such as the right size staples for a foreign-made stapler or a replacement bulb for a flashlight, might not be available locally. Prepare for dust, heat, humidity, and rain. A small canister of compressed air, a soft brush, and some cotton rags (kept dry and clean in sealed plastic bags) can keep a laptop computer functioning for months or years in even the worst of conditions.

Most researchers bring an extra battery pack or two for laptops or other mobile electronics. A remote battery charger can be helpful, too. In especially remote locations, look into solar panels or power sources that plug into a vehicle cigarette lighter, or learn how to rig a recharger from a vehicle battery. Brownouts/blackouts commonly last far beyond the several hours of protection afforded by a couple of battery packs, so do not be surprised by downtime even when you have taken precautions.

Although it may seem obvious, take the time to establish the type of electrical plugs on your equipment and the wall sockets at your site and the appropriate adaptor(s). One of the co-authors failed to notice that his laptop computer had a three-flanged plug, and he brought only two-pronged adaptors. No shop on site carried the necessary adaptor, so he finally called the US and had two seventy-five-cent adaptors sent by a delivery service. It cost sixty dollars and took two weeks, during which time the computer's batteries were, of course, completely exhausted. It later turned out that the US Postal Service's Express Mail service could have delivered the same items in four days at one-quarter the price! So it pays not only to check the details of your equipment carefully, but also to shop around for the most inexpensive and timely means by which to resupply from home, since almost everyone forgets or loses something crucial that cannot be replaced in the field. More generally, one should research the postal situation and establish a reliable method for sending and receiving mail and packages. One can waste a lot of money and lose invaluable information and items on shipping methods well known by locals to be unreliable.

Most researchers need to do some photocopying, be it of archival materials, notes, or questionnaires. When doing bulk work (such as copying questionnaires for a large formal survey), it often pays to arrange a quantity discount with a single vendor. This can provide quicker, cheaper, and more reliable service than just walking in off the street. Also, be aware that copy quality is often poor.

Since all fieldworkers are also tourists of a sort, most bring cameras, whether or not these are central to research design. It is always nice to have shots of your research site for professional presentations as well as for family and friends. One researcher noted, however, that you generally want prints as small gifts to helpful locals. Just because digital photos posted on internet sites, sent to friends' and family members' cell phones, and embedded in PowerPoint presentations are standard for students in North America and Europe, don't forget that few people worldwide enjoy such access. If you use old-fashioned film, or disposable cameras, keep in mind that good quality film developing can be hard to find in some countries. It pays to ask around before delivering a precious roll to an unknown outfit. Otherwise, either arrange with someone at home to process film mailed to them or store used films (in a clean, dry, cool place) until the return home. Also, remember that some film is sensitive to the x-ray equipment used in many developing country airports. Protective lead bags are low-cost, simple preventives.

Equipment does not have to be big or expensive to be important. Some small-sized examples, such as staplers, have already been raised. Mechanical pencils, spare lead, Post-It-notes in all sizes, and clipboards for all research assistants have repeatedly proved indispensable for one co-author's survey work in rural Africa. One contributor suggests, however, buying local pens, stationery and simple office supplies that "people in that setting would not think twice about seeing . . . [i]t is possible that in some small way this strategy will help put your informant[s] at ease." Jerry Shively's testimonial to Ziploc bags demonstrates the importance of some simple items in an especially vivid way.

Box 5.2 Ode to Ziploc bags

The rain was coming at me sideways and even the mongrel dogs had headed for higher ground. It was three days into the trip, and although I thought it was bound to clear up soon, the sun wasn't to appear for another three days. The rain just kept falling.

I had put myself on a fairly tight schedule for data collection in Magsaysay, and there wasn't much room for downtime. Fearing a mutiny by my enumerators, I decided to keep pushing, putting my faith in the Ziplocs. I'm not sure, but I figure I must have been the only person within 1,000 miles with some Ziploc bags. We kept everything in them: the completed surveys, the unfinished surveys, the camera, our dirty socks. Things we needed to keep dry went into them, and things we didn't want to leak went into them. Sometimes we double-bagged just to be sure. I kept my clipboard in one, carefully placing the bag so that I could write inside it. For three days I measured fields with rain pouring off my hat onto a Ziploc bag.

For my money, the two-gallon size is the best: plenty of room, less chance of a rip, and they'll fit on your head, functioning fairly well as a makeshift hat. I'd say take fifty, minimum. If you're going to be in the rough, don't skimp. Get the heavy-duty freezer bags. For dusty conditions, they'll keep your laptop clean. And as gifts to folks in rural areas, almost nothing seems quite as useful; keeping bugs out of the sugar is rural reality.

Jerry Shively

Transportation

You will face some transportation needs in-country. Those working in multiple or especially remote sites will need to pay more attention to transport issues than will those doing archival work in a single city with reliable public transportation. In some areas, the timing of your research affects transportation. Monsoon season turns many non-macadam routes into impassable bogs. Plan accordingly.

It is often true that the simpler you live, the less complex things are. Thus if you live and work in an urban area you may find public transportation a less expensive and time-consuming and more enjoyable and flexible way of moving about than a purchased or rented vehicle. Furthermore, a vehicle creates yet another tangible disparity between you and the subjects of your research. In some circumstances this can be a serious impediment to good research, so consider such possible effects when deciding whether to acquire a vehicle.

Researchers with disabilities face special challenges in many developing country settings. Buses in most developing countries never seem to stop but just slow down a bit for passengers to enter and exit, and are invariably packed with jostling bodies. Trains and subways are not necessarily much better. So public transportation is not always an option for those with special needs. At the same time, private transport is not always superior, since hand-control modifications or other adaptive mechanisms are often unavailable or might not fit the makes of vehicles available on site. More fundamentally, attitudinal barriers regarding the capabilities of disabled persons can be maddeningly ubiquitous. Researchers with disabilities need to make logistical arrangements well in advance to attempt to preempt such difficulties and to prepare for inevitable frustrations.

For researchers working in rural areas, public transport by bus, train, or "bush taxi" can consume enormous amounts of time, and subject you to truly terrifying journeys. Still, many of us delight in our tales of public transport adventure and believe all fieldworkers should experience this, if only once. Unfortunately, local bus and bush taxi systems are often inadequate for getting to and from multiple research sites, especially in remote areas. Also, the more people you need to transport, the more economical and convenient it becomes to have a vehicle of your own.

The expenses of having a vehicle include not just the purchase or rental price but maintenance costs, fuel costs, garaging and insurance. The paperwork requirements for clearing a vehicle, whether shipped from overseas or purchased locally, can also be tedious. As with computers and other research equipment, there is likely to be some sort of import tax on any vehicle brought in from abroad, so budget for that. There is also likely to be a (often high) local registration fee associated with owning a vehicle. There are constant security concerns, and acquisition of a vehicle often gives the researcher unanticipated responsibilities, as we discuss in more detail below. In short, possessing a vehicle abroad entails the same hassles and conveniences – and maybe a few more of each – as at home.

The first choice is what sort of vehicle to use. Bicycles offer not just a means of transport, but a form of exercise as well. As we discussed in Chapter 4, many fieldworkers find regular physical activity crucial to relieving stress and staying healthy. However, cyclists may be less safe on the typically-shoulderless roads of developing countries, especially when competing with seemingly suicidal motorized-vehicle drivers. Furthermore, poorly maintained roads can take a severe toll on all but the sturdiest mountain bikes. Few of those we consulted for this book regularly used bicycles in the field for anything other than exercise or short commuting.

Motorcycles generally handle difficult road conditions far better than bicycles, are often more mobile cross-country than non-four-wheel-drive cars or trucks, and are relatively economical in terms of fuel and maintenance. But, again, there are serious safety issues involved in riding in places where driving customs and laws are considerably more lax than in Europe or North America. There is also the issue of having enough space on the bike to transport necessary equipment. For these reasons, virtually all the researchers we surveyed used a car or truck if they had their own transportation and worked in rural areas. For those based in cities, public transport seems the dominant option for those who are single, a car for those with a family. But scooters are popular with many researchers working in cities, especially in more congested places.

The second choice concerns whether to buy or rent. There is no clear-cut rule as to which approach is least expensive or least risky. A rental offers known but sometimes much higher costs. A good rental company can also offer emergency maintenance support and experienced drivers, which may be of real value. If you buy, vehicle resale prospects are often uncertain. Some respondents report selling their vehicles at or above the original purchase price; they were out only on the cost of fuel and maintenance. On the other hand, one researcher took a hefty loss selling his used car in his agricultural site before his pre-harvest departure; all the locals had their money tied up in unharvested crops. In an unusually extreme case, one contributor not only lost the resale value of his four-wheel-drive vehicle when he was caught in a war zone and his truck was seized by an invading general, but he could not claim the loss from his insurer since the policy did not cover acts of war!

Buying vehicles, especially used ones, takes some skill. First, like car buying in wealthier nations, it is a bargaining sport. If you lack the stomach for such theatrics, prepare to pay a premium. And just like buying a used vehicle at home, unless you are a good mechanic yourself, bring one along to inspect the vehicle thoroughly before you commit to a purchase. A clunker can cost a fortune in maintenance. As one contributor notes, "with a premium on the time to be spent on research, hassling with a lousy car is emphatically not worth it." Other researchers and expatriates in the diplomatic, NGO and multinational corporate communities who are about to leave the country are prime sources for serviceable vehicles and other durable equipment.

Also be forewarned that in some parts of the world (for example, Central America) there is quite active traffic in stolen parts and vehicles. In Nairobi, there is allegedly a place where one can buy back tires stolen off one's car the night before. More seriously, there is always the danger of purchasing a car whose papers appear in order until the police pull you over. One researcher reported knowing someone who swore he repurchased his own car three times after a series of thefts and cross-border migrations!

Assuming you choose a car or truck, certain issues emerge for both purchased and rented vehicles. Do you hire a driver? The expenses involved are obvious – not just the driver's salary, but any additional expenses (lodging, meals) one might need to cover on unusually long trips. Furthermore, a driver means further loss of privacy, which may already be difficult to obtain. The gains from having a driver are freedom from the burden of driving (for those who consider driving a burden), an extra person along when difficulties inevitably arise, and perhaps better contacts for getting spare parts or fuel in areas or at times when such things are scarce. When possible, get a driver who is a skilled mechanic as well. On some fortunate occasions, a driver can offer unanticipated research benefits as well. One of the co-authors found his driver to be an unexpectedly valuable asset in building a sample frame of long-haul transporters and in securing the confidence and cooperation of trucker respondents in a study of food marketing.

Many countries have unreliable distribution systems for fuel, spare parts, and other things necessary to keep a research project going. In such places it often pays to stockpile some basic, relatively inexpensive spare parts (such as hoses, belts, plugs, tires) and fuel. Such a stash must be kept secure. A co-author used a double-locked shed, under a shade tree (to help prevent an explosion when temperatures peaked) and away from his dwelling (in case the fuel blew up anyway – thankfully it did not). When fuel deliveries were interrupted for a week to ten days on three different occasions, the stockpile of fuel in forty-liter cans kept the project on schedule. It also provided an opportunity to build goodwill by refueling a truck and a few motorcycles for a local, non-governmental organization and agricultural extension agents.

Drivers' licenses, although a necessity, are rarely a complication for fieldwork. In the United States you can easily get an international driver's license through any American Automobile Association (AAA) office, which lasts for one year and is renewable. In many countries, a valid driver's license from your home jurisdiction will suffice. Just make sure it does not expire during the field research period.

Maps are essential to anyone traveling through the countryside. While maps are less readily available in stores, gas stations, and the like than in North America or Europe, bookstores and national cartographic agencies usually offer serviceable (if not always current) ones. Be warned, however, that in a few countries maps are still considered security items obtainable only through the military and with proper clearance. Online maps available from Google and other services often provide excellent coverage, and are often more up-to-date than the printed versions available for sale.

Insurance, at least collision and liability coverage, is legally required in many places and a sensible thing to purchase in any case. Before anything happens, know what you need in order to file a claim. Most countries have reliable local insurance vendors who can provide you with a policy suited to your needs and with relatively convenient local claims procedures. There are also international policies available for purchase from home. Check with your own insurance provider or try contacting international insurance brokers. In any case, an insurer with whom you do not already have a relationship will generally require some documentation of your driving record and insurance experience; at a minimum, such paper will win a reduced premium (assuming you have a clean record).

Accidents happen, and in remote areas these can prove serious for even seemingly minor injuries. Airbags are nonexistent and even seat belts are somewhat rare in vehicles obtained in developing countries. Caution is the order of the day on the road. Again, you will appreciate the value of a basic, well-stocked first-aid kit. But even in the fortunate cases where there are no injuries, you may still need to deal with property damages. This process is more or less like that at home, involving insurance companies, the police, and sometimes the court system. Still, the systems often function quite differently from what you might expect based on prior home experience. Resign yourself to spending a seemingly interminable amount of time resolving the administrative and legal matters and repairing your vehicle, if necessary.

A vehicle brings with it many responsibilities. The obvious ones concern maintenance and safe driving. Not so obvious but equally important social responsibilities can emerge when one has a vehicle in areas where few people have access to such a luxury. You will commonly be solicited for rides. In some cases, these will be pedestrians-turned-hitchhikers. Follow your own judgment about this, as you would at home. One contributor had a young man jump into the flatbed of her pickup truck without her permission. He then fell and the researcher bore the responsibility for his medical costs, since the unwritten rule in that location was that "those wealthy enough to have cars should bear responsibility for the passengers, no matter who is to blame for accidents."

Several of us have found ourselves designated (without our prior agreement) as the community supply truck and ambulance. When the local mission priest or the director of the regional schools finds himself out of fuel and the nearest station is one hundred kilometers north, it is invariably the foreign researcher with a truck and fuel cans who is called on to fetch fifty liters. While the opportunity to help is almost surely welcomed, the timing of such requests-cum-demands is often inconvenient. In the end, you just deal with it.

More seriously, health clinics in remote areas are rarely well stocked, so serious illnesses or injuries usually need attention in major cities. A researcher with a vehicle can provide an invaluable service in these circumstances; the bigger the vehicle the better, since whole families often accompany an evacuating member. Of course, it is an inconvenience, consuming considerable time and fuel, and too often includes soiling your vehicle with blood, diarrhea, urine or vomit. But whose research is more important than the health of the subjects of that study or the residents of your host area? Such events provide a dramatic opportunity to give something back to a community from which you are extracting a fair amount, to share the fruits of your privilege, to demonstrate to the community in which you are working that you sincerely care about them and their circumstances, that they are not just so many lab mice in the foreign researchers' eyes.

When serving as ambulance driver, it often pays to stick around the hospital for a bit since a foreign accent may draw more timely treatment. The role of ambulance provider can be a trying one emotionally. Sometimes you are a savior; sometimes you wind up just transporting dead bodies. One researcher comments that such serious and emotional responsibilities are "the single most difficult thing about fieldwork. It is something I can never get used to, and it is the factor that makes me feel most burnt out and in need of a break."

Research assistants

Most overseas field researchers hire someone to assist them at some point in the research project. Assistants are sometimes hired for simple and short-term tasks. Secretarial support for projects such as questionnaire layout or data entry of completed questionnaires can be helpful. Local guides are sometimes necessary to lead you to villages drawn randomly into a survey, since such villages, after all, are inevitably not properly located on one's map and may lie several kilometers' trudge through thick jungle or up a steep escarpment. Other assistants are hired for complex, multi-faceted work over the duration of the project. Common examples include transcription and translation of interviews or survey enumeration.

Whether the employment is short or long term, complex or simple, and with only a few exceptions (e.g. local guides), hiring someone requires not just paying a salary or wage and benefits, but also training and supervision. Carefully weigh the costs and benefits of taking on a research assistant of any sort. One contributor regrets having hired someone in the latter part of his fieldwork:

> This proved not to be worth the effort, since more time and money was spent explaining how to do what it was that I wanted . . . than actual work accomplished. Moreover, since I couldn't pay much, there was little incentive for the assistant to work very conscientiously. Based on this experience, I don't think it makes sense to have a research assistant unless there is ample money budgeted for it. Otherwise, it is simply an exercise in frustration.

If you employ research assistants, the validity of the research project hinges substantially on the quality of their work. You must screen, train and supervise carefully and provide the appropriate incentives, both positive and negative, if you want to complete the project satisfactorily. This is an enormous, sometimes difficult, and often deeply rewarding management experience for which many academic researchers appear quite ill prepared. Many scholars identified the management of research assistants as one of the greatest challenges they faced in the field. Indeed, one person claimed that "logistical and personnel matters may take primacy over academic issues in data collection. . . . Several years' experience in the military was, quite frankly, more valuable to running a good survey than three years' doctoral training."

We cannot overemphasize the importance of the human dimensions of research. Compassion for your enumerators, mutual trust, and patience are necessary ingredients to a successful survey. Careful supervision cannot compensate for a difficult interpersonal climate on the research team. A considerable literature addresses issues of research team composition and dynamics (some of which is identified in the bibliography). We do not pretend that this section covers those matters thoroughly. Our objective here is to call your attention to various administrative, logistical, and human relations questions surrounding the use of field assistants.

If you think you might have use for an assistant, the first questions to ask yourself are for what function(s), and for how long? One contributor hired a full-time research assistant for his one-year project, then added enumerators on an as-needed basis. When you need to conduct interviews in many different languages or when there are short bursts of intense interviewing activity punctuated by longer periods of analysis or archival research, this may be a cost-effective strategy. Think through your specific needs before setting out to find an assistant. Also, consider recruiting and training an alternative or two, especially for larger survey projects.

There is no single best method for recruiting good research assistants. Many researchers rely on recommendations from other researchers (both local and foreign) with experience in the region, from government officials, from host university collaborators, or from non-governmental organizations operating in the area. Some used personal contacts, established in bars, churches, hotels, or restaurants. The process relies as much on serendipity as science.

Once you have identified a pool of interested, prospective research assistants, you need to screen them. Most of our respondents who hired assistants employed the usual devices: a résumé and conversations with or letters from references. Some, especially those who fielded formal surveys, went farther and gave prospective hires a test: for aptitude in filling out a sample questionnaire, for comprehension of the key concepts and terms of the research, or for the ability to think through and resolve difficult interviewing situations. Still others selected a pool of finalists for paid training, then chose assistants and alternates from that trained pool. This is a more expensive and time-consuming approach, but provides a far better chance to observe candidates' behaviors and abilities, both intellectual and interpersonal.

There are no variables that stand out as more important than others in choosing able assistants. The demands of the research design, local cultural mores, and your own skills and financial resources all considerably influence the choice of assistant(s), and in ways that are undoubtedly idiosyncratic to particular projects. Based on the research design, you may have preferences for locals or outsiders, men or women, assistants of a particular religion, or those with special language skills. For those doing formal survey work, the prospective assistants' attention to detail, handwriting, personal appearance, and basic arithmetic skills may be factors to consider as well. The assistants' general attitude, intelligence, work ethic, and sensitivity obviously matter to their likelihood of success, but such things are usually only discovered well into the research project, if at all. You inevitably act on intuition and weak indicators, and should expect to make some hiring mistakes. Having an alternate or two in mind can be handy for when you discover your mistake(s) and provide some peace of mind in the meantime.

Although university students and recent graduates often comprise the bulk of the applicant pool, and foreign students undertaking research are often sympathetic to this group, several researchers were disappointed by the reliability and work ethic of university student assistants. The basic issue appears to be that students often have insufficient time for the intense work schedules of most overseas field research projects, and may not have the maturity necessary to resolve difficult situations. Moreover, in many circumstances university students are outsiders in the communities under investigation – in class, ethnic, and regional terms – and are perceived as such, sometimes degrading their usefulness to the researcher. That said, the pace of work overseas generally differs from that to which workaholics in North American and European universities are accustomed. This can be frustrating but can also provide unexpected insights on the cultural setting and the myriad demands on the residents of your research site. Several contributors remarked that they found married adults to be the most reliable assistants: mature, hard-working, disciplined, but sensitive. Others favored local secondary-school graduates. Familiarity with local customs and dialects is indispensable. Locals often bring with them useful contacts, but sometimes they also carry troublesome relationship histories. There are no clear demographic rules of thumb about who makes a good research assistant, only behavioral ones: you need someone honest, pleasant, patient, responsible, and reasonably intelligent.

Several researchers drew up written contracts laying out the terms of compensation, supervision, conditions of termination by either party, and the period of employment. The researcher and assistant both signed the contract. While such documents might seem rather stiff and formal, they are often necessary to ensure that all parties have a clear understanding of everyone's rights and responsibilities. Indeed, a couple of respondents who struck more informal agreements with assistants came to wish they had formalized the terms of employment.

Incentives matter. One researcher notes wryly that:

> the very structure of doing survey work is such that enumerators have exactly the opposite incentives as the researcher has. The researcher wants to get the job done quickly; the enumerators want it to last as long as possible. The researcher wants good, high-quality data, even if it takes extra effort to get it. The enumerator isn't going to be around to help with data entry, let alone analysis, so has fewer cares about the quality of the data. Nothing demoralizes everybody like having tension between a researcher and his or her enumerators, but they inevitably arise in the course of doing a survey.

In other words, you must explicitly take incentives into account.

The most obvious incentive is the assistant's salary or wage. Several contributors supplemented a fixed regular (monthly, weekly, or daily) stipend with performance bonuses to provide extra incentives for careful work and completion of the project. In addition to individual bonuses based on the researcher's subjective assessment of the quality of an assistant's work, at least one researcher also offered team bonuses for finishing project modules (e.g. the enumeration of a village) on schedule. Another offered a *per diem* bonus for extended periods spent in the field, calculated to be slightly more than an enumerator's necessary expenses so as to induce teams to spend time in survey sites rather than at home in the regional capital. Similarly, several used graduated pay scales, wherein the fixed regular stipend increased over time as the assistant gained experience, presumably becoming more productive and indispensable to the project. This likewise provided inducements to sustained, careful work by the assistants.

Assistants hired for longer periods of time or for hazardous work should be provided with explicit benefits. Just as you need and deserve breaks from the grind of fieldwork, so do assistants. Build some vacation into longer contracts. You may want to build in sick days as well, and plan contingencies for extended illness. Do you pay an assistant full rate, a reduced rate, or not at all when she falls ill or is injured due to no fault of hers or the researcher's? It is hard to know the right thing to do, but you should think through such scenarios and discuss them with your assistant(s). A number of researchers provided health insurance, either through a third-party insurer or on their own, by paying assistants' medical expenses during the project, especially for work-related illness or injury.

Given the enormous importance of good research assistance to most fieldwork projects, it is difficult to compensate good enumerators adequately. While researchers often pay great attention to the monetary benefits offered, bear in mind the non-monetary benefits as well. In many locales, there exists a broader cultural understanding of contractual relations, especially in labor relations, that encompasses symbols of appreciation and loyalty, not just a paycheck or western-style benefits. Pride in the project, respectful treatment by one's colleagues, an opportunity to learn more about a foreign land or language can go a long way toward compensating assistants for hard work on a project of finite duration. Several contributors threw small, regular parties for the research team or paid for rounds of chilled soft drinks in the middle of hot afternoons. Some invested time in writing a formal letter of recommendation that assistants could subsequently use to help gain further work, and some have gone one step further, helping to find post-project employment or academic opportunities for their assistants. One contributor set aside a bit of research money to enroll her research assistants in a computer training class to make them more employable after the project ended.

Research assistants are partners, if sometimes (but not always) junior ones, in the research effort. You can never go wrong giving them due acknowledgment in scholarly books and articles. Some scholars have included assistants as co-authors, and several have sent copies of their final published products back to assistants as a memento of the experience (and a useful tool in landing future research assistantships).

If the research project will take assistants away from their homes, it is your obligation to ensure all team members are adequately housed and fed. Enumerator teams that migrate from village to village will generally need basic supplies such as sleeping mats, a couple of pots, candles, matches, a first-aid kit (including malaria prophylaxis, if needed), a flashlight, and batteries. One of the co-authors used a couple of hundred dollars of grant money to purchase such field equipment, then auctioned all of it off at an end-of-project party, redistributing the proceeds as bonuses to those assistants who completed the project.

Incentives are not the only, or even the major, factor in research assistant performance. Training assistants in an unfamiliar setting and, often, in an unfamiliar language can be a logistical and pedagogical nightmare. It is nonetheless essential to any formal survey work and desirable for many other research methods as well. Not only does a training period permit you to communicate research objectives and the detail of research methods clearly and repeatedly to your assistants, it also helps foster camaraderie among a team that will soon work intensively together. This makes the research experience more fruitful and more enjoyable. If you need hired assistance, it is generally wise to invest the time and resources necessary to train assistants properly before launching into the body of the research project. Aili Tripp emphasizes below the need for mutual input into field research.

Box 5.3 Building partnerships

In working with research assistants, I have found it important to explain the project objectives (I give them my proposal), methods, and what my expectations are of them as assistants. But I also try to find out about their expectations and solicit their advice on the research projects, especially from assistants who have done research before. Since I know I am going to rely heavily on them, I think of them as partners, not simply employees. In the course of the research, I try to create an atmosphere of mutual learning and shared experiences between myself and my assistant(s) and also among them if there is more than one assistant. I have always selected key assistants who were genuinely interested in my research topic and have rarely, if ever, been disappointed. Their work and enthusiasm has often gone beyond the call of duty, and I have been able to benefit from their invaluable insights.

I also try to think of ways in which the research and their contact with me can benefit them beyond simply being a source of income. Much depends on the goals and interests of the individual. One assistant was able to use our findings to write her MA thesis and then went on to pursue a PhD. Another co-authored a paper with me and participated in symposia and roundtables I organized in North America. I did what I could to assist most of them in continuing their education and obtaining further employment.

Aili Tripp

In the ideal, you train assistants to substitute for the lead researcher, so that if you become incapacitated or communications or transport difficulties separate the team, the project can continue apace without any serious degradation in performance. Nonetheless, this ideal is seldom even closely approximated. Among our respondents, assistant training ranged from none at all (which led to a disaster) to a formal, multi-week session of classroom workshops and field testing. Several of us have borrowed a classroom and spent time reviewing interviewing techniques, questionnaire design, coding, variable definitions, translations, the paper trail for questionnaires, and administrative issues regarding pay, transport, lodging, and more. Some researchers conduct the training themselves; others hire locals in whom they have great confidence to direct the training.

Supervision is also crucial if you hope to avoid shirking and sloppiness on the part of enumerators. By no means do we wish to encourage distrust of your assistants. Nevertheless, you must recognize that, as pointed out above, enumerators sometimes have incentives to cut corners, whether due to laziness, a desire to impress or support the researcher, or some other factor. And in many cultures, research is conducted in far more rigid, hierarchical structures than North American and European researchers are used to, so assistants expect to be treated as employees, not colleagues, and are uncomfortable with anything other than a top-down approach. Regular (ideally, daily) spot-checking, built-in validity checks easily incorporated into relational databases in standard software packages such as Access or SPSS, and discussions with respondents about the interviews can be valuable diagnostic tools in establishing whether assistants are following the research design properly. When possible, hold small group meetings in the evening to review the day's data and interviewing experiences while fresh in everyone's mind. This can serve as a valuable exercise in data quality control. As one researcher who ran a complex, year-long survey project in the Sahel noted, "if things don't go well, you can correct mistakes at night and watch for improvement the next day."

If you are prepared to hire assistants, you must also be prepared to fire them, unpleasant as it is. Tolerance of sloppiness can destroy the entire research project. Several researchers reported having to fire assistants, and were often surprised that the dismissals "did not result in any tension in the study village[s]" nor in the team of assistants. Indeed, one of the co-authors has twice had other field assistants express appreciation that a laggard was dismissed, as they felt their colleague reflected badly on them and they were concerned that perhaps the researcher didn't really care about the work enough to set and enforce reasonably high standards.

Research assistants often become longer-term collaborators and life-long friends. Many researchers echoed one person's remark, "I don't know how I would have survived my time in Uganda if I had not been friends with my assistants as well. We socialized together and enjoyed each other's company." Nonetheless, be cautious about mixing friendship with work. The power relationship between the researcher and the assistant is often more complex than it first appears. As locals with advantages of language, contacts, and familiarity with local customs and institutions, assistants can enjoy certain claims and status not possessed by the foreign researcher. The powers of race, wealth, being a guest, and, sometimes, age, nonetheless accrue to the fieldworker. Negotiation of these relationships ranges from congenial and cooperative to competitive to outright conflictive, and cannot be fully anticipated. Pay attention to these relationships.

Several contributors had nightmarish experiences with relationships. One researcher discovered her assistant was in a complicated love triangle involving a member of the household in which she was living. She let the assistant go amid ill-will and embarrassment. Another researcher, who took her assistant in as a housemate (and paid for all the living expenses), encountered conflicts:

My problem was that I had a hard time distinguishing between my roles as employer and friend. I took my job so personally that I found it impossible to work and live with my assistant when we were not getting along. It made it easy for her to make what I felt were unreasonable demands on me, for I just wanted to avoid a big confrontation that would bring my work to a halt. Eventually it became too difficult for us to work together. She was miserable, and had developed health problems as a reaction to her environment. I gave her some money and sent her away. I think we both realized that it wasn't a good idea for us to work together any longer, though I felt really guilty for taking her job away, knowing that jobs are so difficult to find.

As is the case with other logistical and administrative matters surrounding field research, the use of research assistants demands prior planning, patience and flexibility. The joys and trials of your experience, sometimes even the success or failure of the entire venture, often turn on your handling of issues that may seem ancillary to the research project. There are no tried and true recipes for identifying and resolving the myriad logistical challenges of fieldwork. Still, we hope this chapter has been of help in raising important questions, offering useful advice, relaying amusing and instructive experiences, or simply providing an assurance that most researchers endure frustration and embarrassment as a regular – and character-building – part of the experience of fieldwork.

6 Safety and security matters

Doing fieldwork abroad carries with it inherent risks. Unlike work at home in sometimes sheltered campus environments, there is much more uncertainty to deal with on a daily basis, there are different cultural and safety codes to comprehend, and there are usually a great many new stimuli to process simultaneously, to the point where sometimes one's guard is down. Although we caution against the oft-mistaken belief that fieldwork abroad is intrinsically more dangerous than one's day-to-day existence back home, it is essential to recognize that one's familiarity with the risks is typically much less and with less habituation often comes more vulnerability. In this chapter we address security concerns from two different angles to help you anticipate and reduce the risks you run. First, and more importantly, we discuss how to ensure the fieldworker's personal security. Second, we offer some guidance on maintaining security of data and equipment in the field research process itself.

Personal safety: the basics

Safety issues begin with your selection of field sites. While no country is immune to political instability, unless one's objective is to study violence or instability, it is generally unwise to choose as a research site a country known to be unstable or unfriendly towards persons of your nationality, religion, race or gender. With limited time for field research, the difficulties inherent to unstable field conditions magnify the challenges of field research, often at a high cost in terms of one's enjoyment of the experience, the quality of the research, or both. Most colleges and universities have a risk assessment office that can make available information on current conditions and official recommendations regarding travel to any country. Take the time to consult with them early, and then update yourself nearer to the time of your departure.

Many seasoned researchers and international education professionals have a checklist of things to do and not to do while abroad that can significantly decrease your chances of being robbed, assaulted, or worse. Many of these are common-sense recommendations; they bear repeating simply to remind field researchers of what they need to keep in mind before going to the field and what to look out for when they are abroad.

To begin with, before going to the field, make photocopies of any important documents you have, such as passports, credit cards, etc. (some of this basic safety advice is adapted from Middlebury College's Schools Abroad General Handbook). You should leave a copy of everything at home, and also take a copy with you. It is also wise to email yourself a pdf of each of these important documents, leaving the email on a secure server that you can access from wherever you can access email remotely. Find an inconspicuous, secure spot to store hard copies of essential documents such as passports, air tickets, prescriptions for eyeglasses or essential medicines, as well as any small electronics (such as MP3 player, cell phone) or cash. Do not reveal the location to anyone other than your most trusted friend or family member.

You should also think through what you plan to do with your valuables/ valuable documents while in the field. You will not want to put anything of value in a backpack that you might carry around. Backpacks are easy to unzip, and easily sliced open with a razorblade, so they make prime targets for thieves. Fat wallets are easily picked from pockets; if you must carry a wallet in your pocket in crowded areas, at least place it in your front pocket rather than in a back pocket. It is usually much better to carry a smaller bag that you can hang around your neck (and then tuck into clothing) or a money belt hidden under your belt, to the extent that you need to carry any valuables at all while out in public. At a minimum, you will need to carry around some form of identification; you should find out what is acceptable and needed in your research site. It is usually not a good idea to carry around your passport if you can avoid it (though sometimes this is unavoidable, depending on how safe it will be if it is *not* on your person); carrying around a photocopy is obviously much safer.

One researcher suggested, as well, to "make a list of the 3 most important items during the trip (children/family, computer, other research documents) and know where they are at all times." Some researchers will generate a mental checklist – "passport, money, computer, phone, keys" – and will go through that mental checklist on a regular basis, or whenever changing circumstances, leaving a vehicle, going through airport security, etc. We aren't suggesting obsessive/compulsive behavior, but being in unfamiliar environments can distract a person, to the point where important things can easily be forgotten. Make a conscious effort to keep track of your most essential items at all times.

You should always carry emergency numbers with you (or have them memorized). And though you will usually have your keys and a bank automatic teller machine (ATM) card with you, you certainly don't want to carry something that has your address written on it with your keys, or your PIN number with your ATM card. One researcher suggested carrying an ATM card in a place other than a wallet, in a secure place on your body.

When using an ATM card, select a machine in as safe a location as possible. Typically this means away from a corner, shrubbery or other areas where a thief can lurk and surprise you suddenly. ATMs in parking lots filled with cars are especially risky. Try to choose an ATM that is well-lit, with easy visibility – which provides earlier warning of a potential assailant but also creates the perception of more likely detection and the potential for witnesses who might come to your aid. And never accept offers of assistance from strangers at an ATM; go into the bank to ask for help if you need it. If possible, go home as soon as possible after using the ATM machine, so as not to carry around large amounts of cash. When one of the co-authors used to go to a bank to withdraw large amounts of cash for weekly payroll with his field team, he would discreetly bring a guard and transport to get out to the team as quickly and safely as possible with all that money. These are common-sense bits of advice that apply anywhere, but since being abroad usually means you have fewer resources with which to handle potential mishaps, these are especially important to follow when doing fieldwork abroad.

There are other things you can do to avoid being a target of either thieves or people who might be interested in doing you physical harm. For starters, it is not wise to hang out with groups of other foreigners, especially speaking English loudly; in many places, this marks you as a potentially lucrative target. It is also not wise to frequent places that Americans or other foreigners frequent; this can often increase your risk profile. When traveling in a car, be sure to lock the doors and, when driving in areas where you are likely to stop, roll up the windows if the climate permits. If given an opportunity, a city thief will commonly reach through an open window or open a door to snatch a purse, a laptop bag, a backpack or anything else that suggests something valuable lies within. Such grab-and-run events happen far too fast to stop once underway; they must be preempted through precautionary practices.

Avoid wearing clothing or jewelry that will draw attention to you. Sporting an obviously-expensive watch or necklace is more likely to draw interest from a robber than from an attractive prospective date. While you will probably not be able to pass yourself off as a local, you won't want to stand out either. As one researcher who carried out fieldwork as an undergraduate noted, "Remember that you will be perceived differently from the way you may perceive yourself. This is the first key to conducting your own comprehensive risk assessment. It is also important to manage the image you portray by looking critically at the way you appear, what you say, what you do, and most importantly, how it affects others." Stepping outside yourself – or observing other outsiders in the environment where you will be conducting research – is a worthwhile exercise.

You should also consider that given the (probably) unfamiliar environment facing you, you will need to spend a good bit more time and energy on "situational awareness" than you do at home. As one researcher noted, "have a plan B in every situation and try to keep a mental map of wherever you are in relation to identified safe places." Depending on the kind of research you are conducting, you may very well venture into unknown territory. Staying on higher alert than you are accustomed to is helpful when conducting fieldwork, at least in the initial months until you grow comfortable and local mores and patterns become very familiar. This can be exhausting. But you will want to know how to retrace your steps, whatever situations you get into.

Think, as well, about the physical layout of wherever you are staying. A number of experienced researchers point out that when renting an apartment, you may want to avoid the first floor of a building, as these are more likely to be targets of thieves (the same applies in hotels that have less than ideal security). As noted in Chapter 4, you should try to get a good sense of the neighborhoods where you will consider living, and this may take some time (and may require more extensive conversations with locals), so it is best to avoid accepting the first accommodation you find and like, until you know the lay of the land. You will also want to figure out what kinds of taxis are safe, and which are not. In some countries, it is not safe to hail a cab on the street (or at the airport); you may want to rely on more reputable taxi services that are more official and controlled, and it is fairly easy to call a local telephone number to hail a cab. One contributor notes that she was often out late, and had to take cabs home in the wee hours: "I had confidence in my language skills, and so I took that risk. This might sound silly, but I also had an invented 'profile' to share with taxi drivers . . . they tended to ask a lot of biographical information and I really did not want to be rude to someone who was driving me through a foreign city at 4 am." Generally speaking, of course, taking late night cabs does significantly increase one's risk, especially if alcohol is involved. And as implied in the preceding quote, it is wise to be guarded about disclosing personal information to complete strangers.

It's worth noting that many field researchers will probably want to be more leery of strangers than they are accustomed to being. It is perhaps a stereotype, but perhaps accurate: Americans, Australians and a few other cultural groups are more likely to be superficially "friendly" with people whom they meet abroad, and are more likely to be drawn into conversations with total strangers. While sometimes this provides camaraderie and can help you learn more about the place you are studying, it can also be risky. Be wary of overly friendly strangers, who look to be delighted to make the acquaintance of a visitor. Instead, they might be setting a trap, distracting you from your belongings just long enough so that someone else might relieve you of them or learning just enough about you to assess whether a later robbery might prove lucrative.

Fieldwork also often means extensive travel in-country (or between countries), since research projects often take place over a broad geographical space. Because field researchers are often distracted and in unfamiliar surroundings while in transit, it is important to develop strategies for that travel to safeguard belongings and persons. As Annemie Maertens notes, there are many things a researcher can do to minimize risk. Her particular strategies are illustrative.

Box 6.1 Traveling safely

I tried to take the safest means of transportation available and took extra precautions to protect my own safety and that of my belongings. On the trains, I took the upper bed so that I could not be seen from the corridor; I slept on my luggage; on buses I reserved two seats instead of one, especially in the sleepers, or I made sure I had a woman sleeping next to me (making the necessary scene to get this done); I never went out alone after 8–9 pm in the provincial cities. I made sure I established some form of personal contact with the owners of any hostels I stayed in (so they would regard me as part of their family, and hence be somewhat protective). I observed local women, and if I entered a restaurant alone, I made sure there was a section for "families" or that there were women inside.

Annemie Maertens

Here are a few other precautionary (and common-sense) notes. Travel as light as possible; having to haul around heavy bags does not make it easy to deal with suddenly dangerous situations. Don't arrive in an unfamiliar place late at night. Don't go out at night alone, especially to places with which you are not already very familiar. Don't enter train or metro stations at times of day or night when they are likely to be deserted. And if anything serious happens in your research site that might make international news, be in touch immediately with family/friends at home to let them know how you are. Unfortunately, often the only news that makes it home is alarming to loved ones; relieve their anxiety as soon as you can.

Despite one's best efforts, you may well get robbed or burgled. The most important rule is never to confront an attacker who might be armed; give robbers what they demand rather than risk serious injury or worse. Property and money and documents can always be replaced. One of the co-authors had his bag cut multiple times while abroad in Peru, spending time walking through markets where he stood out, although no one ever actually took anything from him, since he wasn't carrying anything of value. If you are robbed, the normal precautions apply: cancel any stolen credit cards immediately, and file police reports, if appropriate. The advisability of dealing with the police varies by country. In some countries, reporting a crime will lead to more hassle and time lost, with virtually no prospect for either recovering any stolen items or catching the perpetrator, in which case it may be better to just let it go. Talk to a trusted local friend or colleague about the best way to handle any such event.

You may also end up with other unexpected problems while abroad. As Carolyn Barnwell notes, it is essential to make sure that someone knows where you are and what you are doing, particularly if you are doing more independent research.

Box 6.2 Keeping people informed

My main strategy is: always tell someone where you are going and what to do in case of emergency.

The last few times I did research abroad, I wasn't affiliated with a particular local university or group. This means no one would have noticed if I didn't show up somewhere for a few days because there was a problem. Being totally independent is sometimes unsafe. You never know when you are going to get sick, stranded, robbed, or just plain lost. If at all possible, always tell someone your rough itinerary and basic emergency contact information.

When I was on Kayangel, the northernmost remote island of the Republic of Palau, I went for a long jog, but forgot to bring a water bottle. I ended up fainting suddenly in front of the governor – who is quadraplegic and couldn't see where I had gone or what had happened, let alone help me. Luckily, I had introduced myself and done an interview with him previously, so he knew my name and who to get in touch with on the island. I was put into a fisherman's boat and taken to the main island to the emergency room where I had my scalp sutured and my host family picked me up from the hospital. I can't imagine what kind of panic and confusion would have occurred if I hadn't told someone in each location some safety information.

Carolyn Barnwell

Less obvious safety strategies

There are as many pieces of safety advice as there are fieldworkers abroad; the preceding section focused on some of the most obvious. But there are also less obvious strategies, especially for more out-of-the-way and dangerous locales, of the sort frequently visited by *New York Times* columnist Nicholas Kristof. Though Kristof's (2009) strategies are typically unnecessary in more secure, middle-income settings, in some more difficult places these techniques – or variants thereof – are very familiar to experienced field researchers:

> Carry a "decoy wallet," so that if you are robbed by bandits with large guns, you have something to hand over. I keep $40 in my decoy wallet, along with an old library card and frequent-flier card. (But don't

begrudge the wallet: when my travel buddy was pickpocketed in Perú, we tried to jump the pickpocket, who turned out to be backed by an entire gang . . .) . . .

Carry a tiny ski lock with a six-foot retractable wire. Use it to lock your backpack to a hotel bed when you're out, or to the rack of a train car. . . .

When it gets dark, always carry a headlamp in your pocket. I learned that from a friend whose hotel in Damascus lost power. He lacked a light but was able to feel his way up the stairs in the dark, find his room and walk in. A couple of final gropes, and he discovered it wasn't his room after all. Unfortunately, it was occupied. . . .

If you're a woman held up in an isolated area, stick out your stomach, pat it and signal that you're pregnant. You might also invest in a cheap wedding band, for imaginary husbands deflect unwanted suitors. . . .

Be wary of accepting drinks from anyone. Robbers sometimes use a date rape drug to knock out their victims – in bars, in trains, in homes. If presented with pre-poured drinks, switch them with your host, cheerfully explaining: "This is an American good luck ritual!" . . .

If you are held up by bandits with large guns, shake hands respectfully with each of your persecutors. It's very important to be polite to people who might kill you. Surprisingly often, child soldiers and other bandits will reciprocate your fake friendliness and settle for some cash rather than everything you possess. I've even had thugs warmly exchange addresses with me, after robbing me. (Kristof, 2009)

In many cases, in the end, a bit of creativity is required when dealing with unusual situations in the field. In the arena of safety, these unusual situations occur more frequently than one might imagine. For example, the problem of drinks spiked with a debilitating drug is increasing, so researchers should be particularly aware of this potential safety concern. Imagining how one might react to a wide variety of unexpected circumstances is probably useful (though by no means should one become obsessive about it), and talking with colleagues who have already had experience in the place where you will be doing your research can be quite helpful.

The sharing of war stories about unusual field experiences is a longstanding ritual among seasoned fieldworkers. Anyone contemplating research abroad would be well-advised to listen to such stories, not just for the entertainment value of the tale, but equally with a thought to "how would I react in this situation? What would be the best course of action if it happened to me?" One particularly good piece of advice comes from Andrew Dillon. He notes the crucial importance of making sure you have as many sources of information as possible when doing research in potentially dangerous areas. Rumors often get out of hand, especially in places where communications infrastructure is not particularly well developed.

Box 6.3 Intelligence gathering in unstable environments

I worked in Northern Mali to conduct my dissertation field research. Northern Mali was a region affected by a civil war in the 1990s with sporadic banditry that continued to the time when I conducted my research. Because banditry was an ever-present issue and cell phone coverage was limited in the Sahara desert, I used several strategies to assure personal security in the field.

The first key to security in the field is making good networks and keeping the lines of communication open with government officials, field staff, and villagers. What's going on in the places you work according to these three groups of informants? Are you getting information from different ethnic groups who may have different sources of information? Personal security is never assured wherever you are in the world, but are the risks manageable? Building relationships with trust will allow you to better assess your security situation. Call ahead to find out what's going on in the next site you are planning to visit and always let multiple sets of colleagues and field staff know your travel plans. Second, make friends with staff at the Embassy and visit with regional security staff. They have the best intra-governmental information available. In the worst case scenario, these would also be the people who would get you out of serious trouble.

During my fieldwork, there were attacks in one area that was proximate to the survey area. There were also rumors that the attacks were going to spread into some of the survey villages and towns. One night, my wife and I were spending the night at the house of one of my field supervisors. There were rumors of an attack on the town and many people, including the governor of the region, military and police fled the town. This left the general population quite scared and closed up in their houses at 4 pm. After discussing with friends in other towns, they suggested we hide our car, which would have been a target for the attacks, and remain in my field supervisor's house, rather than try to move to another village or town, which would have left us exposed and alone along the road. I began to think of where we would hide and which rural areas we could flee to if necessary.

I also called the regional security officer at the US Embassy on his direct cell phone number that he had given me during an introductory meeting before my research began. He alerted me that he hadn't heard about any attacks or police reports of movements of bandits close to my field supervisor's town, but asked me to keep him informed if anything happened and to check in the next day.

Needless to say, there was not much sleep that night, but the rumors turned out to be unfounded. A good communication network meant that I had the maximum amount of information necessary to assess the situation and make the best decisions.

Andrew Dillon

Traffic

While Europeans and North Americans typically worry mainly about risks associated with crime and disease, the greatest risks almost always relate to road travel. As Kristof (2009) puts it, "the scariest people aren't warlords, but drivers." Most experienced field researchers can recall instances in which they took an enormous risk by riding in a car or bus when they probably shouldn't have. One of the co-authors has tragically lost a couple of friends and friends' family members to traffic accidents and violent carjackings. As one contributor notes, when recalling her own experience hiring a car to get around Indian villages: "Have you ever been slalom skiing? Well, imagine doing that with a huge car, and replace the poles with moving trucks, bullock carts, cows, auto-rickshaws, and pushcarts, and throw in a mass of people attempting to cross the ski slope." This is not a pretty picture – although it is commonplace in much of the developing world – and the researcher ended up trying to do more of her travel by train.

It should be obvious, but use a seat belt when at all possible. Many vehicles in developing countries have neither seat belts nor air bags. Many of us have been known to keep a sleeping bag, knapsack or other cushiony article in our lap as makeshift protection in the event of a crash.

When you are in a car with others driving, you will also want to be careful about who you ride with, and the circumstances under which you ride with them. Make sure that whoever is driving can do so safely; the concept of the "designated driver" who remains perfectly sober while friends drink – familiar in North America – is not universal. It is sometimes socially uncomfortable to refuse to ride with someone who appears incapable of driving safely – especially if it might offend your host(s) – but better safe than sorry. If you are able, it may be worth insisting on letting you drive the vehicle yourself. Since manual transmission vehicles are far more commonplace overseas than they are in North America, especially in developing countries, this also implies that it may be worth your while to invest some time in learning to drive a stick-shift vehicle before you head abroad. A few short lessons with a patient friend or family member who is willing to let you learn on his or her vehicle will keep you from having to learn on the fly in a stressful situation abroad.

Keeping research equipment and data safe

Petty larceny is widespread in many places and research equipment such as computers, cameras, and digital recorders are prized targets. And maintaining progress in the research typically depends on safeguarding one's equipment and the data they generate. This can be a challenge in places plagued by widespread petty theft and unreliable electrical systems.

The most basic first step is to lock up equipment whenever possible. Simple, inexpensive cable locks are widely available to secure laptop computers, which are big draws for thieves. Lock computers – even desktop machines and printers or scanners – to something immobile. And lock the room(s) in which equipment is kept when you or an assistant are not physically present.

It is also wise to establish whether your renter's or homeowner's insurance policy covers equipment, especially computers, that might be damaged or stolen overseas. Many companies offer special computer endorsements as additional coverage at low cost. It is wise to check into this option before you leave for the field.

Another reason to keep a close eye on your electronics is that security services are increasingly concerned about tampering with computers and other electronic devices by smugglers and terrorists who, rather than stealing your equipment, might instead tamper with it and leave it for you to carry. Given their appropriate concerns about such matters, airlines and customs services may confiscate your electronics if you cannot be certain that they have been securely in your possession. Karen Booth illustrates the hazards with an especially vivid story.

Besides theft, the other big risks to equipment involve some sort of physical damage. For electronics, the most common problems arise from power

---

Box 6.4 Computers and security

Because of [the Israeli airline's] price and flexibility, I flew to Kenya on El Al. . . . Obviously, El Al has enormous security concerns and a very elaborate and complete surveillance system. When I arrived at New York's JFK airport, I was questioned fully by El Al personnel. I was asked where I packed my bags and if anyone could have gained access to them. With supreme naïveté I told them cheerfully that I had packed them in the home of a friend. I gave my friend's name before I remembered that this was obviously the name of a person of Lebanese descent. That did it. My computer, along with my tape recorder and iron, were confiscated and held in New York while I was given an armed escort to the plane just as it was about to take off. I did not see my computer for four weeks and spent a part of every day at the offices of El Al in Nairobi forcing them to search for this machine. Finally it was discovered that El Al had sent it to the Nairobi airport but had not bothered to let anyone know it was there. In the end I did get my computer and was able to catch up on my work.

I came full circle with my computer experience in the field when four weeks before I was to leave . . . my computer was stolen from my hotel room. I left as I arrived: without computer. The only moral to this story is that one should avoid becoming entirely dependent on a computer and try to anticipate that most things that can go wrong, will!

Karen Booth

surges. Electrical grids in low-income countries and even in older structures in high-income countries are generally far less reliable than on modern college or university campuses. Power spikes and outages are distressingly commonplace. These can corrupt data and software or permanently damage sensitive equipment. A single, brief surge can burn out a computer, cell phone, digital recorder, camera, MP3 player or anything else you might care to carry. So find out the voltage both for your electronics and for the outlets at your site. Many laptop computers and printers today switch automatically between 110 and 220 volts. This very desirable feature has saved more than one jet-lagged researcher from frying his computer when he unthinkingly took a unit last plugged in to a 110-volt system and connected it directly to a 220-volt source. The best safeguard is to buy and religiously use power, telephone and/or all-in-one surge suppressors. These are typically cheaper and of higher quality at home, but they can often be found in electronics stores overseas as well. A power strip surge protector or, better yet, an uninterruptible power supply (UPS) can save equipment from debilitating surges.

Another problem that occasionally arises with electronics and electrical appliances – the coffee maker you brought, a hairdryer, etc. – is that the electrical systems in many residences are not designed for the heavy loads many foreign researchers place on them. Many experienced field researchers have stories to tell of small fires started by plugging in too many devices on a single circuit. One of the co-authors blacked out a lovely old European hotel for an hour after plugging in a phone charger too many. Ask your host or landlord about the electrical system's capacity and carefully identify, one item at a time, how much it can handle safely before you blow a fuse, much less start a fire. And because one of your neighbors or housemates might be less careful than you, invest in a UPS unit for your computer or any other electronic device that you cannot afford to have shut down spontaneously by a power interruption.

Computer viruses can pose a special and severe problem to computer users in developing countries. Perhaps because so much software is pirated, viruses seem unusually commonplace outside Europe and North America. Buy a current copy of good antivirus software, use it and check for updates faithfully – ideally set the software to update automatically whenever you get online – and be cautious about introducing others' USB sticks or CDs into your computer. In a similar vein, be religious about backing up your valuable and irreplaceable material. Such backups can be electronic, hard copy, or both. Also, bring computer startup CDs, which can be extremely useful when software or hardware conflicts occur that prevent the computer from booting up when all the extensions and/or drivers are loaded.

Besides problems caused by electrical spikes or computer viruses, the main risks to equipment relate to physical damage due to working conditions. A small can of compressed air and a straw can do wonders to clean dust out of laptops and other sensitive equipment in dry areas. A well-sealed, waterproof case likewise offers invaluable protection in areas plagued by heavy rains and flooding. None of this will help much if one of your team backs the field truck over the laptop, as happened to one of the co-authors, but short of those sorts of catastrophes, a few simple precautions can carry you far in safeguarding your equipment and data.

While taking proper precautions is essential, Kristof (2009) offers equally essential advice: "Don't be so cautious that you miss the magic of escaping your comfort zone and mingling with local people and staying in their homes. The risks are minimal compared with the wonders of spending time in a small village. . . . And even if everything goes wrong and you are robbed and catch malaria, shrug it off – those are precisely the kinds of authentic interactions with local cultures that, in retrospect, enrich a journey and life itself." We wholeheartedly agree.

7 The challenges of the field

Many texts on research methods deal with technical issues and, as a consequence, are not always useful to a researcher when unpredictable situations crop up, as they often do. You will undoubtedly find yourself confronted with circumstances for which orthodox methods learned from texts or coursework, even research assistantships, are ill suited. First-rate scholarship advances, but the keys to success are likely to be the creativity, perseverance, and training of the researcher.

Not all improvisation is well advised or effective, however. In this chapter, we discuss some issues that are common to many research projects but not usually addressed in methods texts. We do not provide cookbook solutions – many of the experiences we relate are idiosyncratic. We only seek to stimulate thought about how creative solutions can be found to unexpected obstacles. In particular, we address some of the not-so-obvious issues involved in choosing informants, cross-checking data, facing sensitive research topics, and, finally, finding ways to maintain credibility in the field. Throughout this discussion, we consider more informal aspects of research methods, since most researchers reported that "textbooks" were not always helpful given the unpredictable nature of fieldwork.

Choosing and cultivating informants

When you go into the field, one of the first things you have to figure out is who to talk to or who to survey. Since you learn through the people with whom you come into contact, care must be taken in choosing and cultivating informants. That said, there is no single recipe for such selection and no general advice about the best ways to make informants feel comfortable with the researcher. Fieldworkers we surveyed used an extremely wide array of methods to come up with interesting and useful information about their research topics. For example, when doing research focused on political and economic elites, you can usually work out who the important people to interview are by doing an electronic search of newspaper archives and by going to research institutes to find people who may be familiar with your topic of interest. In contrast, if you are working in a rural area, you will quickly need to locate yourself within informal social networks to discover who are the most appropriate informants.

Experienced researchers uniformly emphasize the need to establish solid informal relationships with informants. In some cases this will be much more important than in others. Generally speaking, the anthropologist will need to establish longer-term personal relationships than might a political scientist. Without informal, non-professional contact with informants, the research process is often quite frustrating.

Anthropologist Laura Hammond illustrates the importance of informal contact in describing her method of choosing informants and her treatment of these informants after they had been selected.

Box 7.1 Personal relationships and the research process

One of the objectives of my study was to find out basic household economic information to develop a picture of how returned refugees achieved or failed to achieve self-sufficiency, and to figure out how self-sufficiency was defined. I instinctively felt in the first year of research that I didn't know the people well enough to ask them to participate in an economic survey of this nature. Tigrayans are very secretive about their income, and go to great lengths to hide their wealth from each other (even from other family members) and especially from the local government. I needed to convince people that I didn't work for the government, or the United Nations, and that if I promised to protect their confidentiality, I could be trusted.

To gain the confidence of my respondents, I wrote a one-page letter of consent that I translated into Tigrinya. I read it out loud to each potential respondent household and had the head sign or put his or her thumbprint on it. This letter assured respondents that none of the information they gave me would be used in such a way that they could be identified by it. It said that I would not tell the local government or other community members what kind of information they were providing me with. If they decided at any time that they did not want to participate, or if they decided at some point that they had given information that they wanted to retract, they were free to do so. The letter also stated that they would not derive any direct benefit from participating in the study while it was being conducted. The survey was quite a commitment of time, however, requiring half-hour interviews every day for four months, so I included the promise that at the end of the study I would give them their choice of a goat or sheep as payment. My primary goal in presenting this letter was to cover myself by ensuring that I had the proper consent required by the Committee for the Protection of Human Subjects at the University of Wisconsin, but it was also meant to make them feel that even though they had signed a letter, they had not forfeited their control over participation in the study. No one took advantage of the opportunity to withdraw from the study, but I think that knowing that that option was there and that their confidentiality was guaranteed encouraged respondents to be more honest than they might otherwise have been. When I eventually gave the payment, most respondents said that they had participated out of friendship to me, and that reward was unnecessary, though appreciated.

Laura Hammond

This account emphasizes the importance of considering what will encourage informants to cooperate while remaining within the bounds set by research ethics and institutional review boards. The issue of remunerating respondents has long been contested in the research methods literature, and we do not include this passage as an endorsement of respondent compensation, which some seasoned researchers fear can contaminate data by distorting subjects' behavior. Instead the point is this: Although you might be able identify the best possible informants through diligent research, unless you earn their trust and motivate their participation, you probably will not get very far and your understanding of local circumstances will be limited.

The challenge may be especially acute if your research requires inside information on commercial businesses that go to significant lengths to safeguard proprietary information. As Hope Michelson describes from her work in Nicaragua interviewing supermarket managers, researchers must often strike delicate balances.

Box 7.2 Negotiating access in the corporate world

My project required a significant amount of information from two private businesses operating in Nicaragua, one a multi-national and one a family-owned domestic chain. The information I needed included both descriptions of company operations critical to the qualitative back-story as well [as] complete lists of crops and community names necessary for my survey's sample design. I began with official channels, submitting stamped, sealed and signed letters from my host institution. After some waiting and wrangling I was granted interviews with high-level managers in both companies.

I found these business interviews to be distinct from my meetings with NGO or government officials; business people are generally busy and interviews are likely to be time-constrained and with little time for follow-up questions. There is the added challenge of arguing for your potential usefulness to them – how your work might benefit or interest the company. This can be tough, because the academic papers and studies you will produce are unlikely to be immediately relevant. It may be useful to explain the key points of the research, mapping out how donors or policymakers use potential results. You'll also have to make delicate calculations on the fly – should you push to get everything done in one shot or try to get to know the manager and his staff in case you need to come back later for more.

There is a tricky tension to negotiate when it comes to requesting information through official channels and generating paper trails in the company about your work. For example, I was advised by a colleague not to send an email detailing my work and information requests to the multi-national manager because it could be easily forwarded to senior-level management who might oppose such information sharing.

You also want to be careful to approach the right person in the organization for your initial contact. An upper-level manager may be able to grant you access to the records and financial officers who can help you make sense of them but if your initial interaction with him doesn't go smoothly he's well-positioned to block your access to other institutional channels from the top down. Depending on the type of information you need, a good strategy may be to approach lower-level account managers or regional heads, ingratiating yourself with them over time and ultimately, if necessary, relying on them to bring your case to the higher-ups.

Limited access to proprietary data is a potential third problem. While the domestic retailer worked with me to connect me with individuals who could furnish the details I requested, mapping the information I required from the multinational required a certain amount of legwork and creativity. The multinational carefully guarded its proprietary data and its team of employees required official permission to speak about operations. The multinational manager I interviewed had not authorized me this access. One solution I came up with was to work through my network of contacts to establish a list of former employees for the multinational. Interviewing former employees provided me with lists of municipalities and descriptions of corporate strategies over time.

Hope Michelson

You should also be careful not to give the appearance of "using" informants. This is a tricky business when you think realistically about the research process; after all, most researchers are, in fact, using informants to generate data for their own, academic purposes. You will not get the information sought without their cooperation. We simply point out that you should make sure that the process is not a one-way street. We have more to say about the ways in which you can give something back to informants in subsequent chapters, especially Chapter 10.

That said, keep in mind that some informants will not care whether or not they receive anything back. Public figures, such as government officials, political figures, prominent business people, sometimes even academic "stars," often do not expect or want anything from the researcher. As a consequence, some scholars caution against having high expectations of VIPs. As one political scientist put it, "I discovered quickly that I wasn't going to get much more than the official public statement out of even the ones I had imagined would be relaxed and 'honest.'" Most field researchers have to do quite a bit of digging to find informants who will give useful information and who will not worry about compromising their image.

If you use more formal sampling techniques, you have a different set of worries. Although often concerned with speaking to or surveying individuals, you may not care who these individuals are. Nevertheless, do not assume that random sampling techniques make the research process any easier. As Steve Boucher points out, the struggle to define the sampling frame from which to draw respondents at random can be a serious problem in itself.

Box 7.3 Finding the appropriate sampling frame

In three of my fieldwork experiences I drew formal, random samples. This is a critical stage of research and a stage for which there is usually not formal training. One suggestion, perhaps obvious but nonetheless important, is to define very clearly the unit of analysis. For example, in Mozambique we were interested in analyzing how price liberalization was affecting the dynamism of land markets and the access of low-wealth households to agricultural land. Our principal unit of analysis was the agricultural plot. We needed to find as comprehensive a list as possible of all individual plots in our specific regions. This was perhaps the most time-consuming component of the entire research project. We first needed a random sample of all titled plots. While this was to have been relatively straightforward, in practice it was quite a mess. When I was initially informed that any formal urban or agricultural land must be listed in the Office of Land Registry, I immediately headed there. There I was informed that almost all "titled'" plots were operating without formal title since the process of officializing the title was so time-consuming and expensive that virtually nobody took this last formal step. At that point I thought that the project was finished since our theory regarding the impact of title on land prices had no application in Maputo. Upon further conversation with farmers, however, I became confused because many of those with loans told me that they had used their 'formal' land title as collateral. From there I headed to one of the bank branches to find out what is regarded as sufficiently 'formal' collateral. One bank manager informed me that a document registered in Maputo's municipality was sufficient. Since the plots we were analyzing were in peri-urban zones, the land titling agency was a branch of the offices of the municipality.

After tracking down the functionary responsible for the filing of peri-urban titles, I learned that his office was the last stop in the titling process before the Office of Land Registry. He showed me a very detailed map of all the parcels in the areas we were working in and suggested it would be no problem to randomly choose two hundred out of the five hundred titled parcels, since each parcel was represented by an index card, which were stacked in a corner of his desk.

At this point I was very excited since it seemed that sample selection would be quite easy, but the excitement only lasted until he said, "There's only one little problem." The problem was that in 1991 one of the regions we were working in had been officially transferred to another municipality's jurisdiction. I asked why this was a problem, since the index cards for that area should be in the other municipality's office. The problem, he said, was that when the relocation occurred, a truck came to his office into which some men loaded all documentation related to the areas to be reassigned. 'Why is this a problem?" I asked. Apparently, somewhere between the two municipal offices, the truck got lost and never showed up. Having come this far, I was not about to give up. So I tracked down the official in charge of municipal vehicles to see if he had any suggestions. Unfortunately, that job had been contracted to the military. After several more days I located a military official who had been involved in the incident. After spending some time convincing the official that I really wasn't interested in stealing state secrets, but only in finding lost land titles, he escorted me to several warehouses where low priority documents were stored and said that maybe he remembered something about some municipal documents being dumped here. After sifting through ceiling-high piles of documents I found the missing index cards and was able to draw the sample.

Steve Boucher

If any single lesson can be drawn from this and other experiences, it is that the researcher must be creative and persistent in discovering appropriate informants. Many leads will go nowhere, and adjustments will be necessary during the research process.

Other problems emerge when one is trying to build longitudinal data with repeated observations of the same individuals or households over time. Retracing the original respondents to a past survey can be a time-consuming and often frustrating activity. One of the co-authors endeavored, with local collaborators, to retrace commercial traders previously surveyed in rural market towns in Madagascar four years earlier. But even when providing financial incentives to field enumerators to track down traders who had relocated elsewhere, the team could ultimately find only about one-third of the original sample, effectively undermining the intent to build a panel data set of traders. Another researcher reported how her team struggled to find households surveyed eight years earlier in rural Central America, where addresses are commonly relative to landmarks, such as "500 meters down from the health center" or "close to the old church". Sometimes such structures no longer exist, and the relative location obviously depends on direction of travel. Finding respondents with such cryptic information can take far more time – and fuel and patience! – than one anticipates. This problem is mitigated somewhat as newer data sets typically use handheld global positioning system (GPS) units to record exact locations, although the geographic coordinates and names of respondents are generally treated as confidential information stored in separate files from the core data that is often made publicly available. But retracing past survey respondents remains a challenge for those building longitudinal data sets, even with a GPS in hand.

We also call attention to Boucher's precise definition of the unit of analysis in his work in Mozambique. Many empirical social scientists fail to define precisely their unit(s) of analysis at an early stage and so cast about in an uncoordinated grab at data that ultimately prove difficult, if not impossible, to integrate. This problem often results from the disjuncture common between units of analysis in the theory that informs one's work (for example, association, firm, household, party, state) and the individual unit of inquiry operationalized in most primary data collection. You need to be attentive to, and sometimes creative about, units of analysis in fieldwork.

Cross-checking data

No matter what method is used, you will almost always face a dilemma: How do you know that the information being accumulated is accurate? How do you know that informants are honest? Such questions do not necessarily arise from a suspicion that informants lack integrity. You can imagine, in fact, a wide variety of reasons as to why informants might fudge their answers, or misunderstand question(s). While deception may at times be motivated by a self-interested concern for wealth or reputation, informants might equally fear the political, social, or economic consequences of their words, or they might be telling you what they think you want to hear. Alternatively, your question or accent might be unclear, such that your respondent misunderstands and gives the correct answer to a question other than the one you thought you were asking. Whatever the reason, data errors are widespread in fieldwork and correcting them as best one can is essential if the raw data are to lead to accurate and insightful analyses.

There are various ways to handle these problems. You might enlarge your sample, although this will not help much if the research techniques themselves are flawed. A common and effective way is, as one researcher put it, "the time honored technique of triangulation – in other words, using a number of different methods and sources to obtain the same information – thereby verifying the veracity – or not – of the information." This same researcher noted that an effective way of finding out if you have got the facts right is to share findings with "particularly knowledgeable individuals (e.g. key informants)." An important way to be reasonably sure of getting the right information is through overlapping methods. A mix of qualitative and quantitative methods often provides an effective way to ensure that conclusions bear a fair relationship to reality. In addition, sitting in on the interviews conducted by assistants helps to validate the information assistants reported.

If you have enough time in the field, it may be possible to cross-check data using different methods and repeating your work with a new twist. One scholar discovered the importance of being able to make adjustments in the middle of the research experience, which almost always makes for a more valuable end product:

> I ran a two-round survey, and after the first round of the survey it was clear that the initial case studies had not covered all the territory they should have, so we carried out several more in-between rounds of the survey. At this point, the case studies were less exploratory and more focused on particular topics. After the second round of the survey, we conducted a number of focus group discussions – both with survey respondents and with groups in areas where we had not done any survey work. These turned out to be invaluable, not so much in the sense of providing new data, but in correcting some misinterpretations of case study and survey data, and in offering answers to questions that arose out of survey data.

One of the co-authors has routinely held community workshops to present and discuss survey descriptive statistics after the data have been collected, entered and quickly tabulated and summarized. This informs the host community of basic findings from the study, which is perhaps the most elementary way of "giving something back" to one's research subjects. But these workshops also serve as a valuable quality control check. If the averages and proportions one reports strike the locals as incredible, it is likely that your data have flaws worth searching out carefully. It is far easier to fix such problems while still in the field than months later, once back home at a distant college or university.

Broaching sensitive subjects

In the course of fieldwork, many researchers find – if they were not already aware – that the information they are collecting is very sensitive. The information might be sensitive because it concerns subjects people feel uncomfortable talking about, (such as religious rites, sexuality) or because disclosure could harm the informant (for example, disclosure of illegal activities or taxable wealth). Thinking through the ethics and the research practices associated with protecting your informants is essential. That is the core purpose of institutional review boards. We strongly advise you to study your institution's formal human subjects research guidelines carefully before going to the field and to give thought to these research ethics questions, especially if you are dealing with politically or socially sensitive issues.

You may confront unexpected sensitivity dilemmas. Keep in mind that what an outsider might consider innocuous or mundane may prove extremely sensitive in a particular research context. Aside from possibly causing harm by action or inaction (more on this below), the unexpected sensitivity of certain issues can lead to inaccurate data. One scholar pointed out how this problem of unexpected sensitivity made data collection difficult:

> It was fascinating for me to see how subjects that seemed so neutral to the outsider are in fact quite sensitive to certain informants . . . For example, in asking about food expenditures and intakes, we found two sorts of biases: on the one hand, if informants thought that we were somehow there to "judge" their eating habits, they would tend to exaggerate the data to make it seem as if they were consuming all the things that are supposed to be good for you (meat, vegetables, eggs). On the other hand, if they thought we were there for a handout, they would under-report.

It is important to clarify your data collection objectives and the ultimate use of the data with all respondents before surveying begins. Holding community meetings and hiring enumerators knowledgeable about local conditions and practices can help to accomplish this.

The accuracy of the data can also be affected by who is asking the questions of informants, or even just who is present at an interview. Not only are the outside researcher's race, nationality, gender, and class likely to generate certain assumptions on the part of informants, but local enumerators can affect the way in which informants respond to questions. For example, one of the co-authors found he could not use African enumerators to interview Asian merchants – indeed, the Africans could not even be present during interviews with these respondents – because racial tensions induced blatant misreporting of observable data. Conversely, the researcher had to stay away from some interviews with respondents in areas with particularly painful memories of colonial violence because his race adversely influenced respondents' forthrightness. These were quite unanticipated circumstances and necessitated some creative juggling of surveying schedules and teams.

Beyond the dynamics of researcher/respondent interaction, sometimes the political context can dramatically affect the process of interview and data collection. As a consequence, you must be careful to protect your safety as well as that of your informants. One contributor cautioned that "political situations can evolve very rapidly; what seems fine one year might be very dangerous just a few years later." Particularly in authoritarian regimes, people can and do get killed because of the information they possess, and since the entire research process involves obtaining information, letting the wrong people know when and where you obtained information can be fatal. We emphasize that this is important not only in published research results but during the research process itself, when you may well have conversations with individuals who can harm your informants. Michael Sullivan, who did his work in China, explains how creativity can be employed in sensitive situations.

Box 7.4 Creatively broaching sensitive subjects

My research confronted the problem of broaching sensitive subject matters. I gained the confidence of interviewees through connections with colleagues and friends of theirs. . . . Most interviewees were relatively open to my inquiries, except when it came to politically sensitive subjects. I found that interviewees tended to share their personal thoughts when they were alone with me. Even so, individuals associated with government and party organizations tended to be less forthcoming in their information even if we met privately and in a safe location.

When I met with one interviewee, I found out that he was under semi-house arrest *after* I entered his home. Since he clearly informed me that his house was bugged, we talked about politically sensitive topics with references to Western political philosophy and Imperial Chinese history. The Ming emperor became a hidden way to talk about paramount leader Deng Xiaoping. We had dinner together at a local restaurant. Four security personnel followed us and sat at a table next to us. Rather than talking about democracy in China, he discussed Hegel as a way to criticize Marxism-Leninism and the Chinese Communist Party.

Michael Sullivan

The Chinese case is atypical regarding the lengths to which you must go to protect informants and yourself. More often than not, you can manipulate the research topic to make it sound less threatening. One scholar who worked in Central America in the early 1990s noted that "everything was sensitive. It was obvious that people wouldn't talk to me if they thought I was interested in political issues. I tried to convey the attitude that I was interested in economic policy from a technocratic perspective and that I wanted to talk to them about it technocrat to technocrat. This really worked." Obviously you must be careful that such manipulation does not misrepresent your work, as it might lead to enormous personal and professional complications during or after the fieldwork. Nonetheless, you can usually do some "honest" manipulation of your topic to avoid unnecessary suspicion and noncooperation from informants.

On occasion, you will have to change research topics as a consequence of the sensitivity of the issues being investigated. One respondent recounted, "Early on in my time in Malaysia, I received advice from many sources that it would be difficult and risky to do research on indigenous peoples' movements in East Malaysia. I was advised that I would have to carefully camouflage my real interests" to receive research clearance, and that even if such clearance were obtained, the actual research process would be exceedingly difficult. "All of this convinced me that my original plans would not be feasible without extensive and risky subterfuge on my part." In the end, changing topics to something safer may be the best choice, and most seasoned researchers would agree that it is wise to maintain a flexible research agenda. One of the co-authors routinely cautions students that he has never seen a field research design that was not altered once it encountered the messy reality of the field.

If one is reflective, the challenges posed by the sensitivity of one's research topic can offer important insights that may help soothe some of the frustrations that result from the investigation of sensitive topics. Jason Cons' field narrative offers a wry example.

Box 7.5   The archivist

"You do research on a *sensitive* topic. You won't find any information about it here," the archivist said to me. I had heard this before, many times. "Sensitive" had become the watchword of the first three frustrating months of my historical research on the India–Bangladesh border. This explanation lodged in my mind as simply a polite excuse to deny information and access. Perhaps the only lesson I learned in those early days was to ignore such admonitions and push on. What I could find by doing so was often, if not exactly what I was looking for, at least interesting. So, despite the warning from the archivist,

I blundered around for several weeks making blind requests, searching for information in unlikely places, and trying to understand holding and acquisition indexes. Finally, after weeks of searching, I found a series of files that were relevant to my work. I was thrilled. I went to the same archivist seeking permission to photocopy the materials.

"How many pages do you need to copy?" he asked me. I told him that I wanted to copy perhaps as many as 100–200 pages that day. "Oh, well, that's a problem. You are only allowed to copy 20 pages per day." Frustrated to hear this unwritten and seemingly arbitrary rule, I asked for clarification on archival procedures. The archivist told me, "You see, we always try to help foreign researchers. But, you do research on a *sensitive* topic. I am an archivist, but a citizen of Bangladesh first. I cannot provide you with access to anything that would threaten my country's security." Frustrated, I again asked about additional restrictions. "There are no restrictions", he replied, "You may copy 20 pages a day. As long as they are not secret". "How do I determine if a document is secret?" I asked. Smiling, he told me, "I will decide".

That day, I returned from the archive feeling frustrated and hopeless. As I wrote my field notes about my encounter with the archivist, and several other similar experiences, I began to think. What did this term "sensitivity" mean? How did it work? Why did it keep coming up in my research? What makes places sensitive? How is knowledge about these places produced and regulated? At the time, no easy answers presented themselves. However, the experience led me to think more systematically about what was happening to me as I was conducting research and to use that as data to help understand the spaces I was working on. Over the coming months, these questions emerged as the central questions of my research. Though at the time they frustrated me to the point of tears, treating these research experiences ethnographically ultimately taught me more about my research topic, and provided more productive clues for further investigation, than what I was able to learn from many of the historical documents themselves.

Jason Cons

Recording interviews

If your research methodology requires interviewing informants – and the subject matter involves sensitive issues – you will inevitably confront a crucial question: to record or not to record interviews? There is no consensus among experienced researchers beyond the simple rule that one should never record without the permission of the interviewee. Because of this fundamental disagreement, we simply present the pros and cons of recording and some of the important issues to consider.

Those who favor recording interviews point out that the audio offers an accurate record of the interview itself, and it relieves the researcher of much of the burden of taking notes during the interview. The latter is a particular advantage if note-taking leads you to lose the train of the conversation or eye contact with the interviewee. Especially when interviewing in a foreign language, taping can be very valuable. Having to interrupt the flow of the interview to ask for clarification about a word or phrase can seriously impede the discussion and disrupt the informant's train of thought. If there is an exact record of the interview, you can figure out what was said after the interview is over. Moreover, you might realize some of the subtleties of what was said when listening to the interview a second or third time. Keep in mind, however, that recording usually requires transcription (and perhaps translation) while in the field, since, as one contributor noted, "if you let a large number of interviews pile up . . . the temptation will be too great to simply skip the tedium of getting the data into a usable form."

The case against recording can be made simply: it can substantially distort the interview process. Respondents will be less likely to answer questions honestly if they know there is a permanent record of what they are saying, and thus may tend to be evasive, speak only in generalities, and avoid providing much useful information. The reliability of this assertion depends on the topic under discussion, the demeanor and formal position of the interviewee, and the level of trust. Hopefully, you will be able to sense whether recording will inhibit the informant's responses when asking for permission to record the interview or doing the interview itself. If you sense reticence on the part of the informant, simply ask, "Would you prefer that I turn off the recorder?" This might elicit important information and will signal to the interviewee your sensitivity to his or her situation.

If you do not record the interview, however, you will run into the problem of how to make an accurate record. Some prefer taking notes during the interview, which can lead to the problems mentioned above. And many interviewers record their interpretations and perceptions, which can be easily mistaken later for direct statements made by the respondent. The subtle substitution of interviewer interpretation for interviewee statements is a peril of note-taking in place of direct recording and transcription of discussions. Others prefer to put off taking notes until after the interview is over. A colleague noted that she "did only very discreet note-taking and then immediately ran to the bathroom to jot down the rest." Others prefer to have a recorder with them even when they do not record the interview, because they can quickly recount the dialogue into a recorder immediately after the interview. Either of these techniques requires substantial short-term memory, a trait with which not all of us are blessed.

Finally, we call attention to an important, often overlooked semantic distinction, which can have enormous consequences. Many researchers conflate "confidentiality" with "anonymity" when discussing their approach to sensitive issues. Telling an informant that something is confidential means that the *researcher will not use it* in reporting research results; the information is purely for the researcher's private edification. By contrast, the promise of anonymity simply implies that *the source will not be identified*, but that the information can be used. You must exercise care when using anonymous sources, even where the provider of information has given the researcher permission to use his or her words, if not the individual's name. "Insiders" will often be able to identify the source, which could endanger that individual. On a related note, one researcher said that "even in one's acknowledgments one must be careful not to implicate people simply through their association with a foreign researcher." Once again, think through these ethical issues before going to the field. College and university Institutional Review Boards can provide you with established protocols regarding anonymity and confidentiality.

Giving back and maintaining credibility in the field

Overseas fieldwork is a process of discovery and extraction of information about events, cultures and phenomena native to some place that is (typically) not one's own. This necessarily engenders certain ethical obligations to "give back" something in order to reciprocate for what one extracts. Those who fail to recognize the essentiality of such reciprocity and to act accordingly lose credibility quite quickly – and appropriately – within the host community, and often in the broader research community as well. We likewise caution against conflating research with charitable work; far too many inexperienced field researchers, especially those working in very poor communities, forget the primacy of their role as a researcher.

The concept of academic research is a confusing one for many people (including loved ones, in many cases). Thus, field researchers often struggle with the process of self-definition. This will necessarily change depending on context. You will probably explain your project quite differently to a government bureaucrat than to a landless peasant. Whatever the audience, you need to maintain credibility in the eyes of those in the field site.

The beginning of the research period is often crucial in setting the appropriate tone. One practice that can help establish credibility is to make it clear to respondents and local communities that you will share research results with those who provide the raw data. A sociologist made a strong case for giving something back:

> For both ethical and methodological reasons, research feedback is absolutely imperative. I don't know how many people sighed and agreed to be interviewed but told me they were sure I would just interview them and then run back to [the national university] and never be seen or heard from again. We made a commitment to present our findings to a village

meeting in each one of the enumeration areas – a meeting that not only provoked a lot of good discussion and insight, but also provided a forum to talk about the topic of research in terms of what it meant in the community.

By sharing results with local communities, you create appropriate conditions for an ongoing relationship with those in the research site. You may also help generate goodwill toward other researchers who follow in your wake. Perhaps you will benefit similarly from the good conduct of those who preceded you.

When dealing with an issue that may be considered a development project, expect that many in the research site will assume that you are going to bring money into the local community. This can be a particularly difficult problem to confront, since locals will often not believe protestations that a (relatively) independent researcher cannot bring in money or projects. After all, they often have good reason not to believe what foreigners tell them. The best approach is to make it very clear at the beginning of the research period what you will and will not do for respondents or the community in general. Do not promise anything that you cannot deliver. When you sense ambiguity about how people see your intentions, clarify them.

When at all possible, it is a good idea to figure out a way that the communities in which you will work can derive some direct benefit from your presence, lest you be just a drain on their valuable time. Partly this involves thinking about what information can be useful to the community from your study and how and to whom you might communicate findings in a way that would benefit the community. Such thinking must take place at the design stage. Sometimes this will require collecting information that does not seem directly useful to you but that is obviously beneficial to your hosts and easy to add into your work.

In other cases, this can involve providing material goods. Several surveys one of the co-authors has been involved with have set aside some resources for a community gift: a new generator to replace the broken one at the village water pump, a new classroom for the local school, etc. Sometimes the process of identifying the most valued community contribution can add value to the research, for instance by identifying how and why different groups of people prefer one possible gift over another.

Also be prepared for the occasional unexpected challenges to your credibility. Although some measures can be taken to avoid such challenges, not everything can be foreseen. As excerpts from Carolyn Behrman's journal make abundantly clear, wild and unexpected things happen to the foreign researcher that can threaten the entire project. The individuals mentioned in the story were either research assistants or local friends.

Box 7.6 Handling unexpected challenges to the researcher's credibility

We – Treasure, Futhi and I – set out for the peri-urban community where three of the young women we'd screened at the mother-child clinic lived. The three of them fit our parameters in terms of age, size and age of child, and had said they were interested. The first was a success. In looking for the second woman, we ran into a woman who told us the woman we sought was not there. Our interaction was complicated and oddly hostile. I wanted to locate the correct woman or leave a message for her. Treasure wanted to explain the study to this woman, and Futhi was in a perplexingly aggressive and flippant mood. After a few minutes we left.

We crested the road leading out of this valley and stopped in the local shop for Cokes before returning to our car. Strolling along sipping our drinks, we encountered a taxi driver and a widow from the houses of the community. They told us that we had caused quite a stir. Folks were saying that we were baby-thieves like those described in the papers.

The driver seemed to think the situation was partially funny. The widow was extremely serious. I wanted to return immediately to the community and straighten the mess out but Treasure counseled waiting and Futhi joked with the taxi driver in a way that certainly could have inflamed the situation. We then allowed the two strangers to inspect our car while we appeared to be otherwise occupied. They seemed satisfied that we had no babies on us but stalked around like angry lions and took down the license number. I knew that this was not just going to blow over.

I dropped Treasure off at home and found Zenele in her cool office building and asked her advice. She said to talk to Daniel; he was at home. I buzzed USIS where they helped me make an appointment to be interviewed on the Women's Page of the *Times* of Swaziland to get my name and face and non-threatening activities out there before [more trouble started]. I got [an official] at the US Embassy to write a letter on fancy letterhead that stated very clearly that I was cool.

At home Daniel heard me out and agreed to return to the community with me to clear things up. We took my car and drove straight to the area and parked in the same place. Daniel ran into an acquaintance, the butcher. He advised us that the headman, whom I had consulted days earlier, was not around and suggested we speak with a much-respected retired school teacher.

We found the teacher, and she advised us to return to the original homestead with her granddaughter. At the homestead people began to gather. Daniel, the original woman, and the teacher's husband moved off to talk together. The rest of us formed a loose circle. A nice young guy in a Bahai tee-shirt was conversationally relocated as my occasional translator and defender. But he was teased about being my husband and "had to leave" shortly thereafter. I could hear that Daniel was facing tough opposition. The young woman said she was convinced Futhi, Treasure, and I were the people from an earlier newspaper story about people out to steal children. I was confronted by a group that was occasionally raucous and obstreperous. It became clear that this was half deadly earnest and half entertainment. One woman, who was breastfeeding a one-and-a-half-year-old on demand, went from shrieking at me that I'd come to steal children, slit their throats, and use their body parts for some unspeakably evil purpose to dancing over to me and suggesting that we trade skirts.

The interaction was mainly in siSwati but sometimes the questions came to me in English. Always, the really outraged tones and graphic accusations were directed to me in alternating phrases – first siSwati, then English. The group was trying to make me be evil, to invest me with dangerousness and despicability. It was a struggle of images. I tried to assert my own sense of myself as guileless foreign researcher. Daniel tried to assert [himself as] a . . . slightly aggrandized medical specialist. The process of negotiating my identity rose and fell in intensity but the theme of fierce and offended mothers confronting me was consistent.

Gradually the punctuations in the interaction died down. Daniel and I, together now, continued to insist that I was innocuous and only interested in women's nutrition and work. Daniel twisted my study topic around a bit and told people that I would arrange a time with the headman's wife and come teach about pregnant women's health. The remaining people agreed that that was a good way to end things and the group dispersed.

Carolyn Behrman

Recognize the limitations of your power to change the situation when incidents occur. Behrman reported that one of the local newspapers subsequently ran a story that was favorable to her, while another paper insinuated that she was indeed a baby-snatcher. She said that other researchers "expressed both amusement and discomfort with the apparent random and uncontrollable nature of the incident." The lesson of this story is rather simple: You cannot predict everything that will happen. Hopefully, you will think quickly on your feet when confronted by situations that can undermine credibility. Having local allies available and willing to intercede if necessary proves indispensable to field research efforts more frequently than is commonly acknowledged.

The research process is clearly fraught with uncontrollable situations. We hope, however, that by thinking through – especially *before* the fieldwork begins – the ethics of your conduct in the field, the potential pitfalls of research, and the typical ways in which fieldwork reality deviates from plans, your fieldwork will be both more productive and enjoyable.

8 Knowing when to go home

Like most of the decisions discussed in this volume, there is no universally applicable rule governing the difficult choice of when to pack up and head home. Some fieldworkers have their choices made for them. For one person, kidney failure forced medical evacuation. One contributor, caught unexpectedly in a war zone, recounted, "When I woke to the sound of MIG fighter jets overhead, incoming artillery shells and machine gun fire outside the door I knew it was time to leave!" Only slightly less dramatic, when you run out of money and are directed by authorities to leave the country (or else!), or when your partner (or for graduate students, adviser) says come home *now*, it is almost surely time to pack up. For undergraduates, research is often delineated by the semester program that one studies with, or by the summer between academic semesters.

Many researchers, however, are not forced to leave the field at a precise moment, and many retain considerable discretion over this choice. At some point you have to decide that the data and materials already collected will suffice. Often this realization occurs when you begin hearing (and believing) the same answers over and over again. To be sure, some do not reach such a saturation point for quite a long time. Typically, researchers think that they never have enough information, when in fact it is more often the case that they return with more than they could ever use in a single project. Given that most research projects are more ambitious than feasible, in this chapter we consider questions of planning the last weeks or months in the field, judging what is absolutely necessary for your project, and getting body and data home again safely.

Narrowing the topic

If a clear focus in your field research design does not always pay off in the initial stages of finding funding or beginning fieldwork, it invariably does in the terminal period of the project. Good pre-departure preparations and the exercise of some discipline in the field to stick to the project rather than dash off on alluring tangents, as so many of us do, help immeasurably in getting your research wrapped up successfully and in a timely manner. We are not saying that you must stick with the original research design to the last. Most scholars consulted for this book wisely and successfully changed tack – at least a little – once in the field. But a good sense of the broader literature into which you are trying to fit your research, and of the data and methods necessary to pursue a given issue effectively, substantially improve your prospects for actually getting the right data, in the right ways, and in getting back home relatively quickly to pull it all together.

Several well-prepared researchers recognized quite early during their field research that their original proposals were largely irrelevant. The scholarly literature may be dated, and the information available outside the research site sometimes paints a very different picture of conditions from those you find on the inside. Again, this makes a good case for preparatory research trips, but even these are no guarantee that your research design will prove implementable or sensible when the time comes to launch the project. One researcher suggested:

> it should be anticipated that you will change or narrow the scope of your research topic while in the field – and you should be flexible enough to do this without unnecessary anguish. We cannot help but write inappropriate research proposals or outlines from thousands of miles away (unless we have been there before – another reason for a preparatory trip to the field). For some people a lack of time is likely to be the greatest problem presented by such changes in the field. . . . In general, I think that narrowing the topic as much as possible is essential.

Another political scientist concurred in the absolute necessity of a clearly defined, manageable topic, but cautioned against assuming that you will need to change topics or research design; you run the real risk of perhaps too hastily jettisoning a valid plan on which you worked diligently for some time.

Your original research proposal, revised for changes made in the field, provides an excellent touchstone for narrowing your topic, especially in judiciously choosing how to allocate increasingly scarce resources (not least of which is time) in the waning weeks of fieldwork. For graduate students or established scholars, chapter outlines of the book or dissertation on which you are working can serve a similar end, enabling you to ask yourself, "Can I answer each of the questions raised in this outline?" and "Can I test each of the hypotheses stated?" Direct your final efforts toward those areas that cause you to answer "no" to either of these questions. Undergraduates with less ambitious end products can also ask these same questions, even if the end result is more modest in scope. Undergraduates will often be expected to present results of their research in a public presentation or use their research to write a senior thesis or project, so the end goals will often be the same, even if they are not as extensive.

Many respondents report having been forced to limit the amount of information they collected because they simply did not have as much time to collect, organize and clean data as they had hoped. Ancillary data collection activities (for example, supplementary case studies, secondary data review) are often thrown aside in the end as time runs out. In a formal survey, your flexibility can be sharply limited once the questionnaires are designed and fielded and the sampling plan has been executed. You can often drop a few nonessential questions, but you are largely committed to the program once the survey is fielded. As one economist who fielded a formal survey reported, "A survey with a set body of questions and sampling scheme takes on a life of its own, and if the time and cost necessary are underestimated, it can be very hard to find room for cutting back." Hasty design and implementation of survey instruments have haunted many a social scientist as an unwieldy project dragged on long past the time when grant monies and the field-worker's patience were exhausted.

Clearing the decks

The last days and weeks in the field tend to be frantic. There is so much still to be done, and it is so important emotionally to achieve reasonable closure to this important chapter in your career, personal and professional development, and life. This is an intensely personal part of fieldwork, and can be very positive, as one researcher observed: "I think that last frantic rush before departure is the beauty of the fieldwork experience. Making last-minute contacts, discovering sources and ideas that you wish you'd known months before, saying farewell to friends and to sights and sounds. It was a crucible in which many ideas and intuitions took form. Don't lament the anxiety, revel in it." Most fieldworkers seem to follow and recommend several steps.

The first dilemma you face is what to do with the scarce time remaining. Rest assured, triage is a necessary part of field research. What do you really need to do that is also feasible? Gathering any remaining data unavailable at home usually falls into this category. At the same time, recognize that no one ever gets all the data they think they need, yet somehow good work still gets done. Most fieldworkers develop an expansive sense of what materials are central to the project's success.

Nonetheless, dedicating all your time to data collection is generally not advisable. Data are rarely useful in the raw form in which fieldworkers collect them. Data need cleaning and organizing. This is an explicit part of the process in formal survey work, in which you must enter the data – still typically handwritten onto questionnaires – into some sort of database, and then verify that the entered data make sense. When at all possible, enter the data into the software you intend to store and analyze it in before leaving the field. Making sure that everything is backed up as you are going through this process is essential. Entry and cleaning of field data at this stage permits return visits to the research site to correct errors inevitably identified during entry and cleaning. Double- and triple-check the data, since returning to clean up misrecorded or poorly understood responses is far easier and cheaper when you are in the field than after you have returned home. As Hope Michelson notes, making sure that data is entered properly can save much time and headaches later, and you should take special care to make sure that data entry is done correctly in these final days.

Box 8.1 Don't overlook the data entry

While I planned and consulted carefully when it came to the hiring, management, and payment of our enumerator teams, I gave less consideration to data entry. I hired and trained a group of seven individuals referred to me by my in-country host institutions and I paid them at a set per survey rate. Once I got the digitization up and running, I refocused my attention on the remaining surveying – we had enumerating teams in the field and my daily priority was their management and supervision. Completed surveys went out to digitizers in groups of 20–40; when a digitizer completed his stack he came by my office to trade in the completed set and to upload their recent databases on my computer. I was too focused at that time on tying up loose ends of the data collection to perform more than rudimentary periodic checks on quality of the digitized records. It wasn't until months later when I was back in the United States and fully immersed in the data cleaning that I discovered that two of my digitizers had falsified their records, assigning new observation numbers to already completed records, effectively leaving me with duplicate observations assigned to distinct observation numbers. Between them, two digitizers managed to corrupt nearly 10 percent of my records. Luckily, I had had the original survey hard copies shipped back to the United States, but diagnosing the depth of the problem and paying to have the files re-digitized in the States was extremely expensive in time and money.

I would recommend a systematic approach to data digitization. Treat this last step with the same care and thought that you've put into your collection methods, incorporating rigorous random checks of the data and early critiques with digitizers auditing quality (in the first week or two) as a signal to your team that you are verifying their work. In the future I also plan on using a graduated pay scale, increasing the pay per survey over time as an incentive to maintain quality throughout the job.

Hope Michelson

The end result of field data entry and cleaning is generally a smoother transition from fieldwork to write-up. All the researchers consulted for this volume who finished their PhDs within one year of their return home entered much, if not all, their data in the field, and in many cases began writing at the research site as well. Not only is your data more clearly organized, but you are already launched into analysis, so it becomes easier to advance rapidly after returning home (more on the transition back home in Chapter 9).

Many fieldworkers bring back far more data than they need for the current research project. This can be both a blessing and a curse. On the one hand, the seeds of a subsequent project are already at hand, providing a natural excuse to remain in close contact with host country colleagues. Many of us find parting with new-found colleagues easier when we truly expect to be back soon, working together again. On the other hand, an abundance of data can be a dual burden: logistically, by having to move it all home safely, and intellectually, by taming your desire to master it all before sitting down to complete the project you set out to finish.

Many researchers we consulted indicated that they wanted to leave something tangible behind from their research. Some gave seminar presentations or public lectures at their host research institution and at policy-making institutions before departure, disseminating preliminary research findings locally before polishing them up for presentation to the international academic community. Some host institutions have a working paper series for which you can write a synopsis of your findings as a still more lasting local legacy of your fieldwork. Better yet, you can deposit a copy of your field notes, data set, or both, in a national research institute or library or post them on a website, being sure to inform other researchers where and how to access the material. Host country academics and policymakers, not to mention future fieldworkers, can thereby benefit materially from your project.

For those doing survey work, it is a nice, but too rare, courtesy to present some basic findings in a simple closing talk to the subject community. This can provide useful feedback to the researcher as well as to the subjects. Dan Maxwell went one step further in Uganda.

Box 8.2 Closure with the community

I got some additional funding to organize a day-long workshop, where my assistant and I presented some of our major findings, invited a couple of colleagues to comment on what we had done, and tried to generate some debate on the topic of our research. We invited other members of the research community, policymakers and urban authorities, local political leaders, and a number of the people we had interviewed over the course of the year. . . . The dynamic of the ensuing debate was much different with a number of our respondents present. . . . The spectacle of a well-paid, well-fed expatriate researcher debating urban authorities and policymakers about informal economic practices brings to mind everything that is wrong about foreign researchers (the ivory tower syndrome, academic imperialism, etc.). The spectacle of low-income working women debating local authorities was altogether different, particularly when my data was essentially validating most of the claims the women were making *vis-à-vis* the authorities. Moreover, a number of the analytic insights resulting from that workshop were invaluable.

Dan Maxwell

You need not only to tie up loose ends with your research, but also to attend to personal matters. Closing down your domestic arrangements can take some time. You must either transport home, give away, or sell accumulated household effects and research equipment. Since most returning fieldworkers are burdened with a Herculean load of research materials, local disposal or sending home of any personal effects is often advisable. Often, friends and colleagues will appreciate your leaving behind some of what you brought with you or purchased on site (small furniture, an iPod dock, etc.). Finally, you need to plan well ahead if trying to sell off larger items like a vehicle or a computer. Keep in mind, as well, that selling an automobile (as one of the co-authors did) is often a high-stress process, since dealing in used vehicles is a highly culturally-specific and idiosyncratic practice. If at all possible, bring a local colleague along to help, as you are unlikely to know what you are doing.

In some countries you need to pay attention to currency controls. In a probably futile effort to prevent capital flight, a few countries still restrict the amount of local currency you can take out of the country as well as the amount of local currency you can convert into hard (foreign) currency. In such places, you do not want to show up at the airport with a wad of bills that can neither be taken out (perhaps to be used on a subsequent return) nor converted to a currency useful at home. In this sort of monetary environment, it is wise to manage local currency holdings so as to have little or none left at the end.

Saying goodbye to friends, collaborators, assistants, and the community in which you resided or did research can be emotionally draining and time-consuming. Be sensitive to prevailing local mores. In some cultures, failing to pay your respects immediately prior to departure is a serious slight frequently committed by businesslike westerners. Several respondents threw a party, or offered a community gift as an expression of the bonds of mutual respect forged during the research period.

Packing up the data

The logistical feat of getting your research material home is unnervingly central to the whole intellectual endeavor of fieldwork. Months or years of painstaking work can vanish all too quickly if the proper precautions are not taken in packing and shipping your research materials. It pays to think carefully and early about how the data will get from field site to wherever you plan to complete the analysis and writing, usually at home.

The first question concerns what to take home. Even if all your data have been entered into the computer, cleaned, and carefully reviewed, you should still keep the hard-copy questionnaires and other documents. Marginal notes on questionnaires or passages not originally entered from documents may become important during the write-up. One option – if you do not want to carry all the physical materials back home – is to scan all of the original questionnaires and other documents into pdf files and email them to yourself or post them on an FTP or website or Wiki you can access from home. Be sure to make a backup of all these materials on a USB drive, CDs, or DVDs, just in case disaster strikes. To scan these materials, you can bring with you a small printer/scanner, or use a portable scanner that you bring with you to the field. Finally, all the research materials gathered in the field that cannot be found at home should go back, as should mementos, gifts for family and friends, and personal effects.

The second question concerns how to get everything home and what to do if your well-laid plans go awry. What will you do if the suitcase with all your questionnaires goes not to your destination but to the great luggage carousel in the sky? Take precautions against such low-probability but potentially catastrophic events. Although most fieldworkers never need the backup data sources they create, the peace of mind a backup provides is an important asset in itself. And on the rare occasions when your data are lost or damaged in transit, an effective insurance policy is invaluable.

There are two basic modes of data transport and contingency planning: electronic and physical. For obvious reasons, it is most compact and cost-effective to move data electronically, and it is usually possible to do so except from the most remote locations. You can also leave multiple copies of electronic data at various sites, so that you and others can access it easily if a backup is needed. It is also fairly straightforward and inexpensive to store data on a wide variety of commercial sites, and it may also be easy to store data on your home institution's servers by connecting to those servers remotely through a secure (usually VPN) connection. Working with others collaboratively (with googledocs, for example) is also easy and may help you begin the write-up process while still in the field, if you are working on your project with others.

The more traditional, physical means of transporting data home can be expensive, including the cost of photocopying to insure against loss (more on this below) as well as excess baggage charges. As noted above, scanning such materials and sending them home is a straightforward, albeit time-consuming, solution to the physical transportation of data. Most first-time fieldworkers are shocked at how much *stuff* they acquire in the field, and how expensive and cumbersome it is to ship. If you do have to send things home physically, it is almost always worth the premium to send your research materials home by the safest possible means. Some send boxes of documents as unaccompanied baggage with a courier service or an airline. These services are usually good at tracking down lost items expeditiously. Be aware, however, that travel agents are often unfamiliar with the details of air freight, so it would behove you to visit the airport freight office personally to work out details. The same holds true for seaborne freight in the unlikely event that you send data home by ship. On some rare occasions, you can send materials home with family, friends, or colleagues returning early. Nevertheless, if you are inclined to ask others to help you, be sensitive to the fact that many people are rightly cautious about assuming responsibility for taking others' baggage across borders. Finally, if you are affiliated with the US government in some way (as a Fulbright scholar, for example), inquire whether it will be possible to ship things home via the diplomatic pouch. Back in the old days, before it became common to send things electronically, one of the co-authors had the fortune to get in the good graces of a consular official and was able to ship back eleven boxes of heavy materials (paper and books) free of charge using the diplomatic pouch. However, if you do ship things home, keep in mind that someone must be waiting at the other end to accept the shipment when it arrives. As a consequence, you need to coordinate arrangements for receipt and storage of the material until you are able to claim the baggage yourself.

Most fieldworkers carry most, if not all, their research materials with them on the plane home. This works well for much of what you will bring back, but it does not always work as well for documents and physical specimens. The feasibility of accompanied baggage decreases precipitously, and the expense rises equally quickly, the greater the volume and weight of the materials being sent home. Remember that several boxes of documents can get incredibly heavy. One fellow made it through eighteen months' fieldwork in Sri Lanka without a single injury or illness to speak of, only to break his wrist at the airport at home as he wrestled a pile of overstuffed bags through customs in a severely jet-lagged state.

The day of departure often brings unwanted complications. Perhaps chief among these are conflicts with customs officials. Boxes of books and interview transcripts, and computer and other electronic equipment, may seem innocuous enough, but sometimes raise the suspicions of security-minded customs agents. Especially if your research touches on areas of acute sensitivity in an authoritarian nation, it is unwise to count on a quick and simple clearance through customs. In a panic, some researchers are tempted to resort to bribery. We repeat the advice given in Chapter 4: avoid bribes; they are usually a mistake. Quite aside from the serious ethical questions such actions raise, remember that some officials may interpret an offered bribe as confirmation that the customs agent has reason to be concerned about the contents under question. Thus, bribes commonly backfire in these circumstances. Moreover, the too-conventional view of low- and middle-income countries as rife with corruption cannot be generalized to all officials (and is often inaccurate). One researcher, induced to bribe an airport porter in Los Angeles to clear overweight bags, found it an especially fitting end to his foreign research adventure. "Never a bribe mentioned or paid in Latin America, a land famous for corruption, but an 'enterprising' Los Angeles porter took me for a trip."

If you need to bring home physical specimens – soil or plant material, fossils, etc. – take the time to check out the relevant customs restrictions for both your host and home country well in advance. In the case of agricultural materials (animal, plant or soil specimens), seek technical guidance from your academic adviser on the procedures one must follow to import materials safely and legally. One of the co-authors witnessed the sad spectacle of a young man crying at New York's JFK airport as US Department of Agriculture officials confiscated a box of soil samples he was trying to bring back to his university laboratory without proper permits.

Whatever the means you choose to transport research materials home, it is wise to make copies, at least of irreplaceable original data, for temporary storage elsewhere. Duplication can consume time, energy, money, and storage space. As a result it often pays to find ways to minimize such redundancy. But you run very real risks if you try to save a bit of money by not making duplicate sets of irreplaceable materials. Many researchers leave a duplicate copy of irreplaceable data on site, in the hands of someone trustworthy, who can be contacted if your own copies do not make the trip home satisfactorily. If the data are not yet in final form, leave instructions to destroy the data after confirming the safe arrival of data back home. Others mail a duplicate copy ahead, again relying on someone at home to care for the materials until they can be reclaimed. Replaceable materials need not be duplicated if you ship them ahead early enough to verify their safe arrival before your own departure from the research site.

Finally, while it may be obvious, contingency planning should not wait until you are ready to leave for home. Prudent fieldworkers maintain current backup copies of their data. The laptop stolen from your dwelling or baggage is replaceable, but are the data or initial draft chapters resident on the hard drive? Regular backups and offsite storage of scanned primary documents provide an effective safeguard against calamity.

9 Pulling it all together

The postpartum

Fieldworkers anticipate some turbulence in settling in to a strange place in the field, but few prepare themselves for the shock of reintroduction to the familiar but sometimes unfathomable place from whence they came. Return from the field can be a depressing, disorienting experience for some who come back to their "normal" environments, a soul-searching time for many, and a non-event for others. However you respond to the potential culture shock of returning home after intense weeks, months, or years of fieldwork, you finally confront the need to pull the mass of data together into a manageable project. The initial months are often fraught with both organizational and emotional frustration, as well as the problems associated with becoming reaccustomed to the intellectual environment at home. In this chapter we deal with how to cope with the myriad problems of putting your work in a broader framework, organizing the data, and getting into writing.

Organizing data

For some, the arrangement of data comes only with the process of writing, while for others data organization must precede writing. Most of our respondents fell into the latter group, although this is largely a matter of personal style and chosen research methodology. For those who must organize first, we again strongly suggest not waiting until returning from the field to begin putting data in order. Indeed, the daunting prospect of organizing the data often contributes to the pitfalls outlined in the introduction to this chapter. More than one researcher recommended merging the data analysis, writing, and background research processes as soon as possible. One scholar summed up: "It's crucial to begin writing as soon as possible, I think, because as you write, you find out what you really need to know from the data. And as you look at the data, you find out what you need to write – a dialectical process."

Many fieldworkers spend tireless weeks and months cleaning and re-organizing data files upon their return. Because data cleaning and coding rarely taxes your creative juices, this is often a good activity for the transition period of intellectual resettlement back home. Moreover, the tedium of the process often drives you to start writing.

Data security is still important here. At least one returned fieldworker, still reeling from the elaborate precautions he took to safeguard his data before leaving the field, headed straight for the bank and deposited a copy of his data on diskette in a safe deposit box (back in the day when diskettes were still the preferred method of storage – not *that* long ago!). Do not be lulled into complacency because the electricity supply at home is more reliable than in the field; backing up data and drafts of your thesis or report is still essential.

Beginning (and completing) the writing process

In many ways the key part of fieldwork begins when you start writing. Until that point, the exercise is primarily one of individual enrichment. Once the writing begins, you are able to convert assembled data into a coherent story for a broader audience, making your field site accessible, through print, to the world. The opportunity to share with others what informants and respondents have shared with you is an uncommon one, and you bear a great obligation to tell these stories well and truthfully. For many of us, these fundamental truths about field research provide motivation enough to get writing.

Indeed, some researchers choose to start writing in the field and a few even do all of it there. However, although doing some writing in the field can help the broader project, most researchers need some distance between themselves and their site to gain the perspective necessary to find the patterns running through the various pieces of the research project puzzle. Moreover, few fieldwork projects are purely empirical. Most rest upon a theoretical superstructure and must be placed in a broader literature. The ideal is to find a balance between full integration of theory into your findings and a clumsy graft *ex post facto*. Too much writing in the field can lead to the latter.

Many returned fieldworkers find it difficult to start writing. In some cases, they are adrift in a sea of data. Returning to a central theme of this book, a well-organized prospectus or set of chapter outlines on a clearly circumscribed topic can enable you to find your bearings and get launched. Organizing and cleaning the data as you go along (in the field and at home) can also help in writing. One contributor also cautioned against reading too much before starting writing: "When I returned from the field, I wanted to re-read everything I had read before, and read everything else that I had never gotten around to before I left . . . My adviser finally told me I had to stop, or I would never get any writing done . . . the longer you wait to start just getting things down on paper, the harder it will be to get out of the 'reading trap.'" This is fairly common experience – and good advice – as you know well that there is always something else you *could* read. And of course there is; but it will still be waiting for you after you've begun writing.

In the end, the experience of fieldwork is often overwhelming – usually wonderfully so – and it can take time for you to gain enough perspective on the work to be able to articulate and structure your findings in a coherent manner. Academic pursuits are by their nature somewhat lonesome, as long, hard hours of solitary data analysis, thought, organization, and writing drone on. Having another person around who knows the subject or the site intimately – a partner, a colleague, a friend who studied abroad at the same site, an adviser – can be a great boon, especially in the initial post-return period. Someone else quite familiar with the context, the data, or the issues at hand often helps one find a way to wade through the sea of materials you inevitably bring back from the field.

Motivation problems can be acute in the post-fieldwork phase. Some researchers give themselves clear incentives, positive or negative, to begin and keep writing. Several researchers we consulted committed themselves to present a scholarly paper using their data at a professional conference shortly after their return. Others agreed to write a paper for a soon-to-be-published volume or a book review on a subject closely related to the topic of their field research. Many undergraduates committed themselves to a public presentation of their research upon returning from abroad. A sequence of related talks or papers beginning shortly after your return can provide the impetus and a firm schedule for writing the various chapters in your dissertation, thesis, or monograph. This obviously works best if you started writing or at least scribbling a bit in the field, but even that is not essential. Pride and professional reputation can be powerful motivating instruments; harness them.

For undergraduates, there is often a defined end date for finishing the write-up of one's research, and this is most commonly the senior thesis or project. For many graduate students, the need to find a job inspires disciplined and rapid writing. This seems especially true for those who are supporting families and thus perhaps feel a more acute need to move to the next stage. The job search, especially for academic postings, requires reasonable progress on your work and often a fairly polished paper to offer. The incentives provided by a commitment to present findings from your fieldwork are thus effectively nested within the incentives laid out by throwing yourself into the job market. Keep in mind, however, that a job search is a more pressured undertaking. Do not underestimate the time, energy, and emotion tied up in the search for permanent employment. A job search can stimulate your productivity in finishing off the research project, but it can also take valuable time away from writing. Search for a judicious balance between these two and consult with advisers and loved ones to get input on whether you are ready.

Another motivational strategy, albeit a high-risk one, is to borrow money to support yourself during the write-up phase. Although many of us know of people who were compelled by debts coming due to accept full-time employment before they were ready, putting them on a degenerative spiral, incurring debts can terrify others into remarkable productivity, as Mary Clark recounts.

Box 9.1 Motivating oneself to write

[Writing up] is actually the most painful part of the whole process. It took me a year to figure out that I couldn't get going on writing up my dissertation if I tried to hold down a job at the same time. So, against the advice of everybody I knew, I quit and took out a year's worth of loans. That was a very good decision. Writing up can be tremendously difficult because the dissertation is so big that it's difficult to conceptualize it, let alone know where to start. Taking out loans worked because I couldn't afford to live on debt for more than a year, and so that's exactly how long I gave myself to finish it.

Mary Clark

Most returned fieldworkers begin by writing methodology chapters, bibliographies, lists of data sources, and other detail-intensive accounts from the field, later moving toward more theoretical components of the project. This sequencing serves three useful purposes. First, you can put down on paper important and too-often unrecorded details before time and distance conspire to erase them from your memory. Second, in the initial period back home, the fieldwork experience is familiar, while theory, which most people broadly ignore in the field, seems more alien. In the early weeks back when simple things from daily life – going to the grocery store, reading the newspaper – are often discomforting, there is much to be said for working on material with which you feel (at least temporarily) more comfortable. Third, chapters on field methods, data sources, and descriptive statistics of your data can often be knocked out fairly quickly, giving you a sense of accomplishment and momentum toward the more difficult writing still ahead. Such simple psychological tricks appear repeatedly in researchers' accounts of how they prepared themselves to write up their projects.

Culture shock

Just as you need time to adjust to life in the field, so too do many returned fieldworkers require some time to reacclimate themselves to life at home. Simply put, many experience culture shock at home. Some long desperately to get back on the plane and return to their research site, never to return home again, while others pick up where they left off as if there had never been an interruption. Your emotional response to returning home is a highly individual experience.

Reassimilation can be difficult, in extreme cases even temporarily paralyzing. People's behaviors, the climate, the language, the smells, the food are all different, and not necessarily better or more comfortable. Most likely this is a sign of how substantial the fieldwork experience was, a sure indication that you really need to start writing about this experience. If it is powerful enough to disorient you in your own home, it deserves reporting. The culture shock many feel on reintroduction to home also demonstrates that while fieldwork is explicitly an experience of discovery about some distant place, it is implicitly, but not always subtly, an experience of discovery about things and people quite close, not least about yourself. Often we allow ourselves months or years to process discoveries about our research site(s) but do not permit ourselves even a day to mull over and process what we have learned about ourselves or our homes. This can create a debilitating disequilibrium, to which the best antidote is often to relax, realize such sensations are not uncommon, talk and write about them, and wait it out (and waiting is a practice to which all veteran fieldworkers grow accustomed!).

Although the professional side of virtually all scholars yearns to hit the ground running at home, this is simply not always possible. Culture shock or personal responsibilities may necessitate a hiatus from the project. For example, one of the co-authors took a two-month break to spend time with his pregnant wife and two children after returning from a three-month unaccompanied research trip abroad. Such breaks seem far more common, and perhaps far more sensible, than is commonly acknowledged in the halls of academe. Just as good field research cannot be rushed and must advance in equilibrium with your personal acclimatization, so too must post-fieldwork analysis and write-up proceed deliberately, not hastily. By all means, set about the task of writing, but not at all costs. With luck, your fieldwork experience will be the beginning of a long and fruitful relationship with your site and, more broadly, the practice of fieldwork.

10 Epilogue

It's never over

This book is meant to prepare the researcher for the challenges and joys of fieldwork, to help make the entire process more fruitful. Nevertheless, the narrative would not be complete if we considered a fieldwork project as a discrete event in your life. For many researchers, fieldwork becomes almost addictive, and an initial experience is the start of a career punctuated by substantial periods in the field. But even when you do not obtain or pursue further opportunities to embark on new international projects, time spent in intensive research overseas invariably has durable effects. In this epilogue we briefly discuss some of the post-fieldwork obligations and opportunities that most researchers will confront after they come home.

Post-fieldwork obligations

As anyone who has ever gone to the field knows, the researcher takes a great deal home that represents enormous contributions by others: survey data that required hundreds of hours of time from respondents and field assistants; interview transcripts, tapes, or notes resulting from the time donated by busy people; archival materials that were stored and often organized by people in the field. Many people facilitated access to data, whether by making introductions to informants, providing access to office space or the internet, providing occasional transport, or any of myriad other means. The relationship between the researcher and the researched or those who supported the research is often asymmetrical, and as a researcher, you should do whatever possible to return something to those in the field after you have left. As one contributor said, "I think it is very important to be more than a fleeting presence in a community which one expects to gain some knowledge of. The information belongs there since it is there that it may truly be useful. And it is my responsibility to establish within my means the opportunity for people involved to question or respond to my ideas and conclusions."

At the very least, of course, do no harm to your informants. Institutional review boards have extensive, specific requirements intended to ensure that your research does not jeopardize the wellbeing of others. We have already addressed some of these issues, especially in Chapter 7. Because the principle is so important, and so frequently violated unthinkingly, we repeat and re-emphasize the need to do everything in your power to protect informants. One political scientist, who did archival research, reported:

> My written data exists in a huge gray area. The archivists who provided it to me were uneasy about doing so, but laid down no clear guidelines for its use. I feel an ethical obligation to them to maintain some level of vagueness as to the source of the documents (for example, quoting a document and suggesting that it is in the personal papers of a high-level government official without naming the official, much as I do with the interviews). I also feel obligated to future researchers to make sure I am very careful in the ways in which I incorporate sensitive material. If I use it in a more polemical fashion, or without explaining the full context of the quotes, then I may endanger future access to these documents.

Protecting sources not only safeguards informants against persecution, but may make scholarship easier for those who follow in your footsteps. Exercise careful judgment over what to do with collected information since informants may not necessarily realize the implications of the research project. Which information and identities are and are not sensitive often change over time, sometimes dramatically and in ways unforeseen by the researcher. It is prudent and considerate to err on the side of caution.

If you conduct formal surveys, you also need to be concerned about your data sources, and come up with ways of protecting your sources if you plan to share data with others. One economist wrote that he would "release the data for broader distribution identified only by number, with a separate key containing identifying information only for those researchers who will need to re-interview or match records, possibly asking for a statement agreeing to certain terms of use." As he pointed out, you must be very careful in deciding with whom to share the data obtained. Some researchers have been known to add "noise" to some of the variables in the "unidentified" data set to make sure that individual respondents cannot be identified without consulting the researcher.

Beyond protecting informants, the most tangible and universal obligation is to report accurately and fully what you have learned. Unlike theoretical or conceptual work, in which no one researcher has superior access to the ideas or disciplinary tools necessary to replicate findings, and unlike discourse within the studied community, in which others equally familiar with the issue and the context in which it has been studied can challenge findings, the empirical researcher writing up results at home operates in a sort of safe haven. Findings may be based upon data to which others do not immediately have access, and some of which may not be transferable (such as sensitive information or unrecorded impressions). Because overseas data collection is often an expensive exercise, you bear an obligation to both the scientific and host communities to make data available when at all possible for the purposes of replication and extension. But your primary ethical obligation is to your research subjects; you must protect them first and be clear and generous in reporting on and making data available within the broader scientific community only conditional on your capacity to reasonably safeguard those who enabled you to generate the information.

Most scholars recommend the common practice of sending unpublished or published research results to individuals and institutions in the field. As Hertel *et al.* (2009: 308) write, "exchanging information closes the circle of communicative reciprocity that is the hallmark of socially conscious research. It also helps to get your published work before a wider audience." One economist described some more creative means of sharing her data:

> At the village level, I left behind charts and diagrams summarizing the mean statistics on work and income in that community. For academics and policymakers, I gave two public talks before leaving the field, and I wrote a working paper for the university graduate program, which was printed up and distributed a few months after I left the field. In a follow-up trip to Honduras I revisited three communities to follow up with enumerators.

Many seasoned field researchers routinely offer to give research seminars at host institutions and hold community briefings to disseminate their findings to lay audiences that might take an interest. Such talks can elicit valuable feedback and help deepen relationships for prospective future visits, quite apart from the obvious signal of mutual respect communicated by one taking time to discuss one's work with others who might enjoy and constructively comment on it. Others – especially those working with collaborative projects – will have more formal obligations to share the results of their research.

Sharing data and findings can also lead to possibilities of co-authorship of articles or papers with fellow academics in the field. This can be satisfying for both the researcher and the local academic and is one of the few ways in which the host/researcher relationship can approximate an equal exchange. As one researcher emphasized, "It is essential that researchers realize the importance of treating interviewees and informants as colleagues rather than as simple subjects." Collaboration is one of the best ways to put such a sentiment into practice, since both the local and foreign researcher will produce something tangible, each using his or her particular strengths, contacts, and accumulated knowledge.

A word of caution is in order at this point. Although you may want to share your research, contacts, and resources with those with whom you work in the field, be careful about making promises, whether academic or financial. Making promises you cannot keep can damage your own credibility, as well as that of other researchers who in the future might contact those with whom you worked. Furthermore, as Gretchen Bauer notes, future relationships with informants can become complicated after you leave the field, especially when you had close contact with the research subjects. In particular, political factors might limit what you can do in the future.

Box 10.1 Fieldwork as an ongoing process

I became rather closely involved with the trade union community in particular in Namibia and with many Namibians in general. I feel that I will have an ongoing relationship with both well into the future. I came to work with the trade unions as a researcher doing research on them but also for them as we grappled with the trade unions' own research capacity in an independent Namibia. In such situations one should always be careful not to promise more than one can deliver. One should never make any commitments that one does not intend to or cannot fill. To do so would be to enhance people's expectations falsely and would be very wrong. At this early stage I am not exactly sure how my relationship with the trade unionists and other informants will develop in the future. In large part this is because of the way in which the whole issue of the trade unions has become so politicized and the way in which any foreigners who might be attempting to influence the trade unions (e.g. to disaffiliate from the ruling party) are being viewed by the authorities. For the time being, I feel that I need to move away from the unions and perhaps attempt other research in Namibia.

Gretchen Bauer

Bauer underlines the point that the researcher should regard the fieldwork as an ongoing process and not a one-shot deal. We heartily endorse that perspective.

Post-fieldwork opportunities

While fieldwork encumbers you with obligations to do no harm to informants and respondents, to report stories accurately and fully, and to make data available to the broader scientific community when at all possible, it also provides uncommon personal and professional opportunities. They include the social opportunities associated with new and often lifelong friendships. They also involve numerous professional opportunities, ranging from the possibility of advising others as an "expert" on your research topic or place to opportunities to expand further on your original research project, either in the same country or elsewhere. In short, overseas research pays permanent dividends to those blessed with the chance to do it. We hasten to add that one may see obligations turn into opportunities, for example, with the chance to co-author an article with a researcher from your field site.

Ken Wilson (1993: 198) succinctly summarized several of the most important and tangible benefits of fieldwork:

> Fieldwork is for life. Friendships and responsibilities are created that will stay with you forever. Many researchers still correspond with people from the area they worked in decades later. Several have made follow-up studies, a re-engagement that catapulted them back into the personal relationships of previous years. A few researchers have never made the break and ended up abandoning academia altogether and going back to live with the people they studied.

Opportunities for consultancies or contract research often appear following an intensive fieldwork period overseas. Research institutions and policy-makers value experience. No matter how ignorant you might feel when you return home overwhelmed with data and impressions gathered but not fully analyzed or synthesized in the field, an astonishing number of people rightly label returned fieldworkers "experts" in the area. You may be able to take advantage of this newly acquired status. For example, one scholar we spoke with turned her fieldwork experience into an opportunity to go back to "her" country on a USAID mission. Upon her return to the field, she was able to renew old contacts and verify and refine some of her earlier conclusions.

Many scholars use their field experience to begin new research projects. Often, such extensions involve research in neighboring countries and allow a more comparative project with potentially broader implications, in which you ask similar research questions in a different context. Having proven that you could execute the research in one place makes you less of a risk for potential funders. Therefore, emphasize previous research experiences when attempting to secure new funding. You can also use field contacts to begin a new project on a related theme. For example, one of the co-authors used his initial experience in Brazil studying trade policy as a stepping stone for a broader research project on South American economic integration. The initial research experience made this new project possible. It provided contacts, knowledge of resources, and a familiarity with the local context that made it possible to ask more appropriate research questions.

Finally, you can return to the field to do follow-up research in the same site. Longitudinal studies over the span of many years remain quite rare. The ability to return to a site and replicate the study after the passage of time is a methodological option unavailable to most scholars. If done properly, this can be an extremely valuable intellectual contribution.

Overseas fieldwork is a complicated and challenging process. Some of the challenges are random and unique, depending on the particularities of individual countries; others are predictable. In this book we have concentrated on the latter, operating on the premise that fieldwork will go much more smoothly if you take steps to prepare for some typical challenges. Nonetheless, it is essential to maintain flexibility and to appreciate that each field research experience is unique and deeply personal, often as a result of serendipitous events. As we noted in the introduction, the fieldwork process is a (sometimes absurd!) sequence of decision points. In this book we have tried to give you the benefit of the substantial experience of many who have already gone through the process, through the difficulties, and through the satisfaction of the truly rare experience of going abroad and trying to understand a foreign culture. Overseas research is a uniquely enriching dimension of academic life; seize the opportunity and enjoy it to its fullest.

Selected bibliography

In this selected bibliography we provide a broad compendium, not a comprehensive listing, of relevant materials on overseas research. Many of the references were taken from the "recommended readings" bibliography prepared for the Social Science Research Council's International Predissertation Fellowship Program, which ran for roughly a decade from the early 1990s. Others references were provided by the co-authors, contributors, reviewers and others who reviewed the manuscript.

Archival research

Elder, G. H., E. K. Pavalko, and E. Colerick Clipp. 1993. *Working with Archival Data: Studying Lives*. Newbury Park, Calif.: Sage Publications.

Hill, M. R. 1993. *Archival Strategies and Techniques*. Newbury Park, Calif.: Sage Publications.

Scott, J. 1990. *A Matter of Record: Documentary Sources in Social Research*. Cambridge, Mass.: Basil Blackwell.

Weeks, J. M. 1991. *Introduction to Library Research in Anthropology*. Boulder, Colo.: Westview Press.

Westerman, R. C. 1994. *Fieldwork in the Library: A Guide to Research in Anthropology and Related Area Studies*. Chicago, Ill.: American Library Association.

Case study research and comparative method

Achen, C., and D. Snidal. 1989. "Rational Deterrence Theory and Comparative Case Studies." *World Politics* 41: 143–69.

Dogan, M., and D. Pelassy. 1984. *How to Compare Nations: Strategies in Comparative Politics*. Chatham, N.J.: Chatham House Publishers.

Eckstein, H. 1975. "Case Study and Theory in Political Science." In F. I. Greenstein and N. W. Polsby, eds, *Strategies of Inquiry*, Reading, Mass.: Addison-Wesley.

Geddes, B. 1990. "How the Cases You Choose Affect the Answers You Get: Selection Bias in Comparative Politics." *Political Analysis* 2: 131–49.

Kanbur, R., ed. 2003. *Q-Squared: Combining Qualitative and Quantitative Methods of Poverty Appraisal*. Delhi: Permanent Black.

Lieberson, S. 1991. "Small N's and Big Conclusions: An Examination of the Reasoning in Comparative Studies Based on a Small N of Cases." *Social Forces* 70: 307–20.

Lijphart, A. 1975. "The Comparable-Cases Strategy in Comparative Research." *Comparative Political Studies* 8: 158–77.

Ragin, C. 1987. *The Comparative Method*. Berkeley: University of California Press.

Tilly, C. 1984. *Big Structures, Large Processes, Huge Comparisons*. New York: Russell Sage Foundation.

Yin, R. K. 1988. *Case Study Research: Design and Methods*. Newbury Park, Calif.: Sage Publications.

Ethnographic methods and qualitative research on human subjects

Agar, M. 1980. *The Professional Stranger: An Informal Introduction to Ethnography*. New York: Academic Press.

Asad, J. 1973. *Anthropology and the Colonial Encounter*. New York: Humanities Press.

Barley, N. 1983. *The Innocent Anthropologist*. London: British Museum Publications.

Barnes, J. A. 1979. *Who Should Know What? Social Science, Privacy, and Ethics*. New York and Cambridge: Cambridge University Press.

Bartis, P. 1990. *Folklife and Fieldwork: A Layman's Introduction to Field Techniques*, rev. edn. Washington, D.C.: Library of Congress.

Bell, D., P. Caplan, and W. J. Karim, eds. 1993. *Gendered Fields: Women, Men, and Ethnography*. London and New York: Routledge.

Brown, R. H., ed. 1992. *Writing the Social Text: Poetics and Politics in Social Science Discourse*. New York: A. de Gruyter.

Burgess, R., ed. 1982. *Field Research: A Source Book and Field Manual*. New York: Routledge, Chapman and Hall.

Clifford, J., and G. E. Marcus. 1986. *Writing Culture: The Poetics and Politics of Ethnography*. Berkeley: University of California Press.

Consortium on Qualitative Research Methods. Online at http://www.maxwell.syr. edu/moynihan/programs/cqrm/

Devereux, S. 1993. "'Observers Are Worried': Learning the Language and Counting the People in Northeast Ghana." In S. Devereux and J. Hoddinott, eds, *Fieldwork in Developing Countries*. Boulder, Colo.: Lynne Rienner.

Dexter, L. 1970. *Elite and Specialized Interviewing*. Evanston, Ill.: Northwestern University Press.

Douglas, J. D. 1985. *Creative Interviewing*. Beverly Hills: Sage Publications.

Ellen, R. F. 1984. *Ethnographic Research: A Guide to General Conduct*. New York: Academic Press.

Ely, M. 1991. *Doing Qualitative Research: Circles within Circles*. London and New York: Falmer Press.

Emerson, R. M., R. I. Fretz, and L. L. Shaw. 1995. *Writing Ethnographic Fieldnotes*. Chicago: University of Chicago Press.

Faubion, J. D., and G. E. Marcus, eds, 2009. *Fieldwork is Not What It Used to Be: Learning Anthropology's Method in a Time of Transition*. Ithaca, NY: Cornell University Press.

Finnegan, R. H. 1992. *Oral Traditions and the Verbal Arts: A Guide to Research Practices*. London and New York: Routledge.

Fox, R. G. 1991. *Recapturing Anthropology: Working in the Present*. Santa Fe: School of American Research Press (distributed by University of Washington Press).

Geertz, C. 1988. *Works and Lives: The Anthropologist as Author*. Stanford, Calif.: Stanford University Press.

Gladwin, C. H. 1989. *Ethnographic Decision Tree Modeling*. Newbury Park, Calif.: Sage Publications.

Golde, P., ed. 1986. *Women in the Field: Anthropological Experiences*, 2nd edn. Berkeley: University of California Press.

Gravel, P. B., and R. B. M. Ridinger. 1988. *Anthropological Fieldwork: An Annotated Bibliography*. New York: Garland Press.

Hammersley, M. 1995. *Ethnography: Principles in Practice*, 2nd edn. London and New York: Routledge.

Ives, E. D. 1995. *The Tape-Recorded Interview: A Manual for Field Workers in Folklore and Oral History*, 2nd edn. Knoxville: University of Tennessee Press.

Jackson, B. 1987. *Fieldwork*. Urbana: University of Illinois Press.

Jorgensen, D. L. 1989. *Participant Observation: A Methodology for Human Studies*. Newbury Park, Calif.: Sage Publications.

Lee, R. M. 1995. *Dangerous Fieldwork*. Thousand Oaks, Calif.: Sage Publications.

Lofland, J., and L. H. Lofland. 1994. *Analyzing Social Settings: A Guide to Qualitative Observation and Analysis, Third Edition*. Florence, KY: Wadsworth Publishing.

Malinowski, B. 1989 [1967]. *A Diary in the Strict Sense of the Term*. Stanford, Calif.: Stanford University Press.

Moran, E. F. 1995. *The Comparative Analysis of Human Societies: Toward Common Standards for Data Collection and Reporting*. Boulder, Colo.: Lynne Rienner.

Moris, J., and J. Copestake. 1993. *Qualitative Enquiry for Rural Development: A Review*. London: Intermediate Technology Publications, Overseas Development Institute.

Nordstrom, C., and A. C. G. M. Robben. 1995. *Fieldwork under Fire: Contemporary Studies of Violence and Survival*. Berkeley: University of California Press.

Panini, M. N., ed. 1991. *From the Female Eye: Accounts of Women Fieldworkers Studying their Own Communities*. Delhi: Hindustan Publishing.

Pelto, G., and P. Pelto. 1978. *Anthropological Research: The Structure of Inquiry*, 2nd edn. New York: Cambridge University Press.

Pfohl, J. 1986. *Participatory Evaluation: A User's Guide*. New York: PACT Publications.

Punch, M. 1986. *The Politics and Ethics of Fieldwork*. Newbury Park, Calif.: Sage Publications.

Rosaldo, M., and L. Lamphere. 1974. *Woman, Culture, and Society*. Stanford, Calif.: Stanford University Press.

Rosaldo, R. 1993. *Culture and Truth: The Remaking of Social Analysis*. Boston: Beacon Press.

Sanjek, R. 1990. *Fieldnotes: The Makings of Anthropology*. Ithaca, NY: Cornell University Press.

Schoepfle, M., and O. Werner. 1987. *Systematic Fieldwork*. Newbury Park, Calif.: Sage Publications.

Shaffir, W. B., and R. A. Stebbins, eds. 1991. *Experiencing Fieldwork: An Inside View of Qualitative Research*. Newbury Park, Calif.: Sage Publications.

Spradley, J. P. 1979. *The Ethnographic Interview*. New York: Holt, Rinehart and Winston.

—— 1980. *Participant Observation*. New York: Holt, Rinehart and Winston.

Stocking, G. W., Jr. 1983. *Observers Observed: Essays on Ethnographic Fieldwork*. Madison: University of Wisconsin Press.

Stouthamer-Loeber, M., and W. B. van Kammen. 1995. *Data Collection and Management : A Practical Guide*. Thousand Oaks, Calif.: Sage Publications.

Van Maanen, J. 1988. *Tales of the Field: On Writing Ethnography*. Chicago: University of Chicago Press.

—— ed. 1995. *Representation in Ethnography*. Thousand Oaks, Calif.: Sage Publications.

Warren, C. A. B. 1988. *Gender Issues in Field Research*. Newbury Park, Calif.: Sage Publications.

Weiss, R. 1995. *Learning from Strangers: The Art and Method of Qualitative Interview Studies*. New York: Free Press.

Whitehead, T. L., and M. E. Conaway, eds. 1986. *Self, Sex, and Gender in Cross-Cultural Fieldwork*. Urbana: University of Illinois Press.

Zamora, M. D., and B. B. Erring, eds. 1986. *Human Intervention: Fieldwork in Cultural Anthropology*. Trondheim, Norway: Dept. of Social Anthropology, University of Trondheim (publication of the Association of Third World Anthropologists).

Fieldwork in general

Ackroyd, S., and J. A. Hughes. 1981. *Data Collection in Context*. London: Longman.

Aldrich, D. P. 2009. " The 800-Pound *Gaijin* in the Room: Strategies and Tactics for Conducting Fieldwork in Japan and Abroad," *PS: Political Science and Politics* 42(2): 299–304.

Barley, N. 1983. *The Innocent Anthropologist: Notes from a Mud Hut*. New York: Penguin.

Barnes, J. A. 1977. *The Ethics of Inquiry in Social Science*. Oxford: Oxford University Press.

Bauer, D. G. 1995. *The "How To" Grants Manual*. Phoenix: Oryx Press.

Burgess, R. G. 1984. *In The Field: An Introduction to Field Research*. Boston: George Allen & Unwin.

Corbridge, S., and E. Mawdsley. 2003. "The Practices of Fieldwork" special issue of the *Singapore Journal of Tropical Geography* 24(2).

Devereux, S., and J. Hoddinott, eds. 1993. *Fieldwork in Developing Countries*. Boulder, Colo.: Lynne Rienner.

DeVita, P. R. 1992. *The Naked Anthropologist: Tales from Around the World*. Belmont, Calif.: Wadsworth Publishing.

Freilich, M., ed. 1977. *Marginal Natives at Work: Anthropologists in the Field*. New York: John Wiley & Sons.

Golden, M. P., ed. 1976. *The Research Experience*. Itasca, Ill.: F. E. Peacock.

Hertel, S., and M. M. Singer. 2009. "Field Research in Developing Countries: Hitting the Road Running," *PS: Political Science and Politics* 42(2): 305–9.

Kristof, N. 2009. Cum Laude in Evading Bandits. *New York Times*, May 31, 2009.

Mikkelsen, B. 2005. *Methods for Development Work and Research: A New Guide for Practitioners*. Thousand Oaks, CA: Sage Publications.

Myrdal, G. 1969. *Objectivity in Social Research*. New York: Pantheon Books.

Ortbals, C. D., and M. E. Rincker, eds. 2009. Fieldwork, Identities, and Intersectionality: Negotiating Gender, Race, Class, Religion, Nationality, and Age in the Research Field Abroad. Special issue of *PS: Political Science and Politics* 42(2): 287–90.

Penslar, R. L. 1994. *Research Ethics: Cases and Materials*. Bloomington: Indiana University Press.

Perecman, E., and S. Curran, eds. 2006. *A Handbook for Social Science Research: Essays and Bibliographic Sources on Research Design and Methods*. Thousand Oaks, CA: Sage Publications.

Rabinow, P. 1977. *Reflections on Fieldwork in Morocco*. Berkeley: University of California Press.

Razavi, S. 1993. "Fieldwork in a Familiar Setting: The Role of Politics at the National, Community and Household Levels." in S. Devereux and J. Hoddinott, eds, *Fieldwork in Developing Countries*. Boulder, Colo.: Lynne Rienner.

Reinhardt, G. Y. 2009. "I Don't Know Monica Lewinsky, and I'm Not in the CIA. Now How about that Interview?" *PS: Political Science and Politics* 42(2): 295–8.

Robson, E., and K. Willis. 1997. *Postgraduate Fieldwork in Developing Areas* Developing Areas Research Group Monograph No. 9. London: University of London.

Scheyvens, R., and D. Storey, eds. 2003. *Development Fieldwork: A Practical Guide*. Thousand Oaks, CA: Sage Publications.

Smith, C. D., and W. Kornblum, eds. 1989. *In The Field: Readings on the Field Research Experience*. New York: Praeger.

Whitehead, T. L., and M. E. Conway. 1986. *Self, Sex and Gender in Cross-Cultural Fieldwork*. Urbana: University of Illinois Press.

Wilson, K. 1993. "Thinking about the Ethics of Fieldwork." In S. Devereux and J. Hoddinott, eds, *Fieldwork in Developing Countries*. Boulder, Colo.: Lynne Rienner.

Grantswriting

Browning, B. A. 2008. *Grant Writing for Dummies, Third Edition*. New York: John Wiley & Sons.

Pzreworski, A., and Salomon, F. 1998. *The Art of Writing Proposals*. New York: Social Science Research Council.

Yang, O. O. 2005. *Guide to Effective Grant Writing: How to Write an Effective NIH Grant Application*. New York: Springer.

Living abroad

Albright, S., A. Chu, and L. Austin. 1993. *Moving and Living Abroad: A Complete Handbook for Families,* rev. S. Albright and C. deKay Wilson. New York: Hippocrene Books.

Cassell, J. 1987. *Children in the Field: Anthropological Experiences*. Philadelphia: Temple University Press.

Kohls, L. R. 1995. *Survival Kit for Overseas Living: For Americans Planning to Live and Work Abroad*. Yarmouth, Maine: Intercultural Press.

Rose, S. R. 1994. *International Travel Health Guide*. Northhampton, Mass.: Travel Medicine (annual publication).

Schroeder, D. G. 1993. *Staying Healthy in Asia, Africa, and Latin America*, 3rd edn. Chico, Calif.: Moon Publications.

U.S. Department of State. 1994. *Security Guidelines for American Families Living Abroad*. Washington, D.C.: U.S. Dept. of State, Overseas Security Advisory Council.

Weller, C. N. 1995. *The Overseas Assignment: A Professional's Guide for Working in Developing Countries*. Tulsa, Okla.: PennWell Books.

Werner, D., with C. Thurman and J. Maxwell. 1992. *Where There Is No Doctor*. Palo Alto, Calif.: Hesperian Foundation.

Quantitative methods

Agresti, A., and B. Finlay. 1986. *Statistical Methods for the Social Sciences*. Riverside, N. J.: Dellen/Macmillan Publishing.

Amemiya, T. 1987. *Advanced Econometrics*. Cambridge: Harvard University Press.

Berndt, E. 1991. *The Practice of Econometrics, Classic and Contemporary*. Reading, Mass.: Addison-Wesley.

Box, G. E. P., and G. M. Jenkins. 1984. *Time Series Analysis: Forecasting and Control*, 2nd edn. San Francisco: Holden Day.

Dubois, J.-L. 1992. *Think before Measuring: Methodological Innovation for the Collection and Analysis of Statistical Data*. Washington, D.C.: World Bank.

Ethridge, D. 1995. *Research Methodology in Applied Economics: Understanding, Planning, and Conducting Economic Research*. Ames: Iowa State University Press.

Freedman, D., R. Pisani, R. Purves, and A. Adhikari. 1991. *Statistics*, 2nd edn. New York: Norton.

Gebremedhin, T. G., and L. G. Tweeten. 1994. *Research Methods and Communication in the Social Sciences*. Westport, Conn.: Praeger.

Greene, W. 1990. *Econometric Analysis*. New York: Macmillan.

Harvey, A. 1990. *The Econometric Analysis of Time Series*. New York: Philip Plan.

Hoel, P. 1984. *Introduction to Mathematical Statistics*, 5th ed. New York: Wiley.

Judge, G. G., R. Carter, and W. E. Hill. 1988. *Introduction to the Theory and Practice of Econometrics*, 2nd edn. New York: Wiley.

Nachmias, D., and C. Nachmias. 1987. *Research Methods in the Social Sciences*, 3rd ed. New York: St. Martin's Press.

Neuman, W. L. 1994. *Social Research Methods: Qualitative and Quantitative Approaches*. Boston: Allyn & Bacon.

Research ethics

DeVries, R., D. A. DeBruin, and G. Goodgame. 2004. "Ethics Review of Social, Behavioral, and Economic Research: Where should we go from here?" *Ethics and Behavior* 14(4): 351–68.

Pace, C. A., and E. J. Emanuel. 2005. "The ethics of research in developing countries: assessing voluntariness" *The Lancet* 365 (9453): 11–12.

Panel on Institutional Review Boards, Surveys and Social Science Research, National Research Council of National Academies. 2003. *Protecting Participants and Facilitating Social and Behavioral Sciences Research*. Washington: National Academies Press.

Penslar, R. L. 1995. *Research Ethics: Cases and Materials*. Bloomington, IN: Indiana University Press.

Scheyvens, R., and H. Leslie. 2000. "Gender, Ethics and Empowerment: Dilemmas of Development Fieldwork," *Women's Studies International Forum* 23 (1): 119–30.

Study abroad

The Forum on Education Abroad. 2008. *Standards of Good Practice For Education Abroad (3rd edition)*. Carlisle, PA: The Forum on Education Abroad.

Institute of International Education. 1998. *Open Doors 1998: Report on International Educational* Exchange. New York: Institute of International Education.

Institute of International Education. 2008. *Open Doors 2008: Report on International Educational Exchange*. New York: Institute of International Education.

Survey research

Ashby, J. A. 1990. *Evaluating Technology with Farmers: A Handbook*. Cali, Colombia: CIAT.

Belbase, K. P. 1991. "Rural Household Data Collection in Developing Countries: Designing Instruments for Collecting General Household Information Data." Cornell University Working Paper in Agricultural Economics 91–13. Ithaca, NY.

Booker, W., P. Singh, and L. Savane. 1980. "Household Survey Experience In Africa." Living Standards Measurement Study Working Paper 6. Washington, D.C.: World Bank.

Casley, D. J., and D. A. Lury. 1981. *Data Collection in Developing Countries*. Oxford: Oxford University Press.

Converse, J., and S. Presser. 1986. *Survey Questions: Handcrafting the Standardized Questionnaire*. Beverly Hills, Calif.: Sage Publications.

Freedman, D., A.Thornton, D. Camburn, D. Alwin, and L. Young-Demarco. 1988. "The Life History Calendar: A Technique for Collecting Retrospective Data." In *Sociological Methodology* 18: 37–68.

Grootaert, C. 1982. "The Conceptual Basis of Measures of Household Welfare and Their Implied Survey Data Requirements." Living Standards Measurement Study Working Paper 19. Washington, D.C.: World Bank.

Grootaert, C., and K. F. Cheung. "Household Expenditure Surveys: Some Methodological Issues." Living Standards Measurement Study Working Paper 22. Washington, D.C.: World Bank.

Grosh, M., and P. Glewwe, eds. 2000. *Designing Household Survey Questionnaires for Developing Countries: Lessons from 15 years of the Living Standards Measurement Study*. 3 volumes. Washington: World Bank.

Johnson, A. C., Jr., and J. S. Rowe. 1987. *Agricultural Statistics for Developing Countries*. Madison: University of Wisconsin.

Kalton, G. 1986. *Introduction to Survey Sampling*. Beverly Hills: Sage Publications.

Kiecolt, K. J., and L. E. Nathan. 1985. *Secondary Analysis of Survey Data*. Sage University Paper, Quantitative Applications in the Social Sciences No. 07–053.

Kumar, K. 1989. "Conducting Key Informant Interviews in Developing Countries." USAID Program Design and Evaluation Methodology Report 13. Washington, D.C.: USAID.

Leones, J. P. 1991. "Rural Household Data Collection in Developing Countries: Designing Instruments and Methods for Collecting Time Allocation Data." Cornell University Working Paper in Agricultural Economics 91–16. Ithaca, NY.

Leones, J. P., and S. Rozelle. 1991. "Rural Household Data Collection in Developing Countries: Designing Instruments and Methods for Collecting Off-Farm Income Data." Cornell University Working Paper in Agricultural Economics 91–18. Ithaca, NY.

Levin, C. 1991. "Rural Household Data Collection in Developing Countries: Designing Instruments and Methods for Collecting Consumption and Expenditure Data." Cornell University Working Paper in Agricultural Economics 91–14. Ithaca, NY.

Lipton, M., and M. Moore. 1972. "The Methodology of Village Studies in Less Developed Countries." Discussion Paper Number 10. Sussex, Eng.: Institute of Development Studies.

Longhurst, R. 1981. "Research Methodology and Rural Economy in Northern Nigeria." In *IDS Bulletin,* vol. 12: 23–31. Sussex, Eng.: Institute of Development Studies.

Low, J. W. 1991. "Rural Household Data Collection in Developing Countries: Designing Instruments and Methods for Collecting Health and Nutrition Data." Cornell University Working Paper in Agricultural Economics 91–15. Ithaca, NY.

Poate, C. D., and P. F. Daplyn. 1993. *Data For Agrarian Development.* Cambridge: Cambridge University Press.

Randolph, T. 1991. "Rural Household Data Collection in Developing Countries: Preparing the Data for Analysis." Cornell University Working Paper in Agricultural Economics 91–19. Ithaca, NY.

Rossi, P., J. D. Wright, and A. B. Anderson. 1983. *Handbook of Survey Research.* Orlando, Fla.: Academic Press.

Rozelle, S. 1991. "Rural Household Data Collection in Developing Countries: Designing Instruments and Methods for Collecting Farm Production Data." Cornell University Working Paper in Agricultural Economics 91–17. Ithaca, NY.

Scott, C., P. T.A. de Andre, and R. Chander. 1980. "Conducting Surveys in Developing Countries: Practical Problems and Experience in Brazil, Malaysia, and the Philippines." Living Standards Measurement Study Working Paper 5. Washington, D.C.: World Bank.

Smith, L. C., and A. Subandoro. 2007. *Measuring Food Security Using Household Expenditure Surveys.* Washington: International Food Policy Research Institute.

Sudman, S., and N. M. Bradburn. 1982. *Asking Questions: A Practical Guide to Questionnaire Design.* San Francisco: Jossey-Bass.

Tatian, P. A. 1992. *Designing a Data Entry and Verification System.* Washington, D.C.: International Food Policy Research Institute.

Von Braun, J., and D. Puetz, eds. 1993. *Data Need for Food Policy in Developing Countries: New Directions for Household Surveys.* Washington, D.C.: International Food Policy Research Institute.

Weisberg, H., and B. D. Bowen. 1977. *An Introduction to Survey Research and Data Analysis.* San Francisco: W. H. Freeman.

Wood, G. D., Jr., and J. A. Knight. 1985. "The Collection of Price Data for the Measurement of Living Standards." Living Standards Measurement Study Working Paper 21. Washington, D.C.: World Bank.

Index

marriage certificates 41
Marxism-Leninism 111
MAs 3, 87
Maxwell, Dan 74, 124–5
mechanics 79–80
medication 33
medicine 33, 91
meetings 88
men 39, 42, 60–2, 84
methodology 1–2, 21, 46, 115, 132, 138
Michelson, Hope 104–5, 123
microphones 37
Middle East 3
migration 7, 11, 79, 86
military 80, 83, 97, 107
Minnesota 55
misinterpretation 109
misrepresentation 112
mobility clauses 22
modems 37
moisturizer 36
money 27–30, 53–6, 82, 86, 89; challenges 116, 120; going home 120, 123, 128; postpartum 131; security 91–2, 94
money belts 91
monitors 73
monographs 131
monsoon seasons 77
moonlighting 26
Morarji, Karuna 56–8
Moroccans 71
Morocco 13
mosquito nets 31–2
mosquitoes 30, 32–3
motivation 131–2
motorcycles 79
Mozambique 106, 108
MP3 players 91, 100
multinational corporations 41, 57, 79, 104–5
music 12, 38
Muslims 40, 42

NAFSA 42
Nairobi 48–9, 79, 99
Namibia 51–2, 75, 137
Narayanan, Sudha 10
narrowing topics 120–2
nationality 110
networks 54, 67, 97, 103
New Delhi 57
New Year 52

New York 60, 99, 128
newspapers 16, 52, 54, 57, 67, 102, 117–18
NGOs 3, 34, 79–80, 83, 104
noise 135
North Africa 65
North America 7, 12, 15, 18, 74–6; logistics 79–80, 87; security 98, 100
North Americans 41, 61, 84, 88, 98
note-taking 114
novels 38

obligations 134–8
observation 68
Oceania 3
Office of Land Registry 106–7
office supplies 77
officials 44, 58, 64–5, 74, 83, 105–7, 127–8, 135
opportunities 137–9
Ortbals, C.D. 62

packing 35–40
Palau 95
papers 131, 136
Paprocki, Kasia 25–6, 65–6
parasites 32
participation rates 6–7
partners 45, 86–7, 120, 131
passion 11–12
passports 34, 91
patience 26, 68–9, 71, 75, 83, 89, 122
payment 103–4, 123
Peace Corps 11, 55
pediatricians 33–4
pens 77
pepper spray 37
peripherals 72–3
permission 113
permits 128
personal relationships 103–4
personal safety 90–5
personnel 83
Perú 94, 97
PhDs 3, 8, 87, 124
Philippines 32, 72
philosophy 111
phone cards 45
phone numbers 16
phones 14, 16, 20, 29, 35; logistics 71–3, 76; preparations 37, 41, 43, 45; security 91, 97, 100
photocopies 14, 39, 44, 72–3, 76, 91, 113, 126